Money Karma

Money Karma

The Essence of Financial Happiness

Katherine Lee Bonnett
& Jonathan E. Bonnett

Hardie Grant Books

Disclaimer

All financial details and statistics are based on information available at the time of going to press. The authors and publisher accept no responsibility or liability in the preparation or advice given that results in damage, injury or loss herein to any person or corporation. The names and identities of the people in the book have been changed to protect their privacy. Any resemblance to persons living or dead is a coincidence.

Published in 2003
by Hardie Grant Books
12 Claremont Street
South Yarra, Victoria 3141, Australia
www.hardiegrant.com.au

All rights reserved. No part of this publication may be reproduced, stored in a retrieval system or transmitted in any form by any means, electronic, mechanical, photocopying, recording or otherwise, without the prior written permission of the publishers and copyright holders.

The moral right of the authors has been asserted.

Copyright © Katherine Lee Bonnett & Jonathan E. Bonnett 2003

National Library of Australia Cataloguing-in-Publication Data:

Bonnett, Katherine.
  Money karma: the essence of financial happiness.
  ISBN 1 74066 025 0.
  1. Finance, Personal – Religious aspects – Buddhism. 2. Finance, Personal – Psychological aspects. I. Bonnett, Jonathan. II. Title.

332.024.

Edited by Jane Fitzpatrick
Cover and text design by Andrew Cunningham, Studio Pazzo
Typeset by Studio Pazzo
Printed and bound in Australia by Griffin Press

Every effort has been made to incorporate correct information and statistics. The publishers regret any errors and omissions, and invite readers to contribute up-to-date or additional relevant information to Hardie Grant Books.

10 9 8 7 6 5 4 3 2 1

*This book is dedicated to the reader:
may you find personal and financial happiness*

Contents

Introduction		1
1	The Journey to Financial Enlightenment and Happiness	9
2	The Subconscious Mind and Its Power	21
3	Budgeting	37
4	Debt Wisdom	55
5	Gambling	77
6	Relationships	85
7	Investing	103
8	Ethical Investing	125
9	Women and Finance	135
10	Retirement Planning	157
11	The Baby Boomers' Financial Awakening	163
	Achieving Money Karma	195
	Glossary	199
	Sources	203
	Acknowledgements	205
	Index	207

Happiness

May you have
Enough happiness
to keep you smiling
Enough trials
to keep you strong
Enough sorrow
to keep you human
Enough hope
to keep you happy
Enough failure
to keep you humble
Enough success
to keep you eager
Enough friends
to give you comfort
Enough enthusiasm
to look forward
Enough faith
to banish depression
Enough determination
to make each day
better than yesterday.

ANONYMOUS

In this book we use the term 'happiness' to describe what you try to reach for in your life. In no way do we intend to suggest that you can spend your life experiencing extreme happiness at all times. Money Karma is about experiencing life with its ups and downs without the added burden of money or debt problems. It is also about understanding that your search for happiness can not be undertaken merely by spending money and accumulating materialistic objects. It is about understanding who you are and what can make your time on this earth worthy and peaceful.

Money Karma Journey to Enlightenment

The journey to enlightenment involves the inter-relationship between physical, spiritual and social elements and it requires us to balance many areas within our lives. To get the right balance requires a commitment to self-discipline.

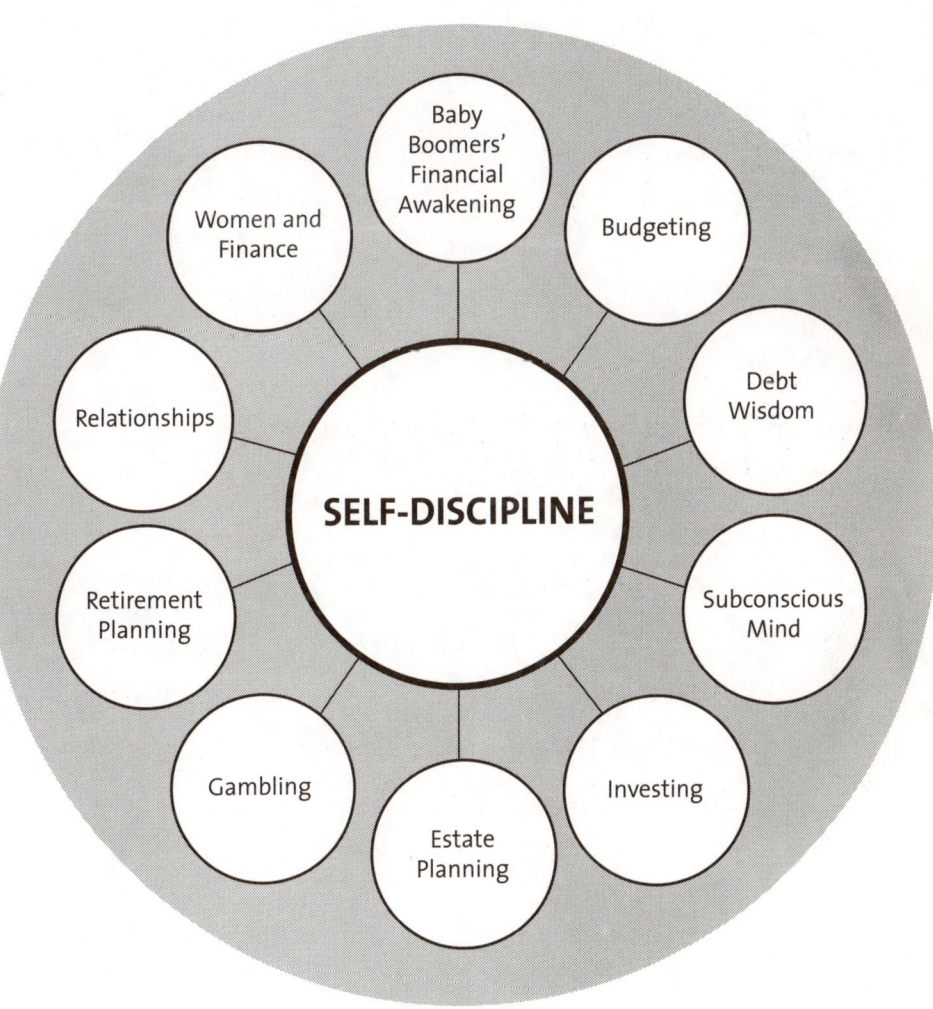

Introduction

What do you really want from your life? Believe in yourself and you will achieve it.

Money Karma is the energy surrounding the way you manage financial aspects of your life. It is an energy unique to you. We all have individual life experiences, personalities and needs. Understanding Money Karma means that you understand the way you consciously choose to spend your money. We often fail to recognise that we are the keepers of our own financial security. Instead of examining our own actions, we go in search of an answer that will free us from our financial situation.

> *The thing you really believe in always happens ... and the belief makes it happen.*
> — FRANK LLOYD WRIGHT

This book will help you re-examine the way you look at managing financial and personal aspects of your life. To understand Money Karma you need to develop a holistic approach involving all the elements of your life, visualising where you want to go. If you can't see it, it won't happen.

Read each chapter, noting ideas you need to revisit and investigate further. Write down what you feel is missing from your life – this is now your list of things to reach for. With persistence and patience you will be amazed at how your financial situation changes.

To introduce positive Money Karma into your life, you'll have to learn to examine how happiness is often measured. Most of us constantly focus on external influences, instead of understanding that self-discipline is one of the keys to happiness, and that being undisciplined can only lead to negative outcomes. You'll also see that success will not come to those who only focus on the financial aspects of their life.

If you are living a life consumed with negative financial energy, you are creating negative Money Karma. To overcome this you need to bring balance back into your life. Take into consideration all aspects of your life and discover why you are constantly burdened with money problems. Sometimes we are warned that there is an imbalance in our lives by stressful events that happen around us. These warnings may act as a wake-up call, urging us to examine an aspect of our life that we are neglecting. When these warnings relate to bad Money Karma, it is time to take positive action to rectify the imbalance. There are many external factors that can influence how you manage the financial aspect of your life, but if you recognise the negative external influences you will not allow negative karma into your life. You are the master of your financial destiny, and you can empower yourself to honour your responsibilities. You should always be aware of how your actions are going to affect the balance of energy in your life.

> *Education's purpose is to replace an empty mind with an open one.*
> — MALCOLM S. FORBES

This book offers useful strategies, techniques, principles and worksheets to assist you to discover what is important in your life. It will show you how to implement these strategies in your life. *Money Karma* aims to help readers facing difficult situations by providing a variety of solutions specific to their circumstances.

Money Karma shows how you can:

- achieve financial success by setting realistic goals
- develop mortgage reduction strategies
- live the life you want now and in retirement by developing holistic savings strategies
- achieve financial goals if you are single, married, in a relationship, divorced, widowed or a step-parent
- examine your overall health and fitness levels to limit financial hardship as you age
- plan for unforeseen circumstances (injury, unemployment or illness)
- implement a Baby Boomer Budget for retirement planning
- prepare for family planning issues
- achieve financial happiness for women, whether in a relationship or single
- identify and control gambling problems
- devise ethical investment strategies
- implement the No Fail Money Karma Budget Plan (page 41) and plan for your future financial security.

The basis of this work includes some personal lessons from Buddhist philosophies used in our daily life. We are not Buddhist, but find some of its spiritual lessons easily integrated into our beliefs. We hope no Buddhist or philosophical purists will take offence at the use of some Zen terminology, but will see how these Zen ideas are an integral part of our existence. Goodness, patience, tolerance and kindness can only benefit humanity. It is these principles on how you conduct your life positively that we believe are important.

Money Karma was written for people struggling with the demands of work, home life and money management. Jonathan realised that many of his clients' money management issues related to their lifestyle choices. These clients needed to create a lifestyle more satisfying than their present choice: one that included activities adding to the quality and purpose of their lives. Integral to this was the development and implementation of an easy-to-manage budget.

A budget is like a window into your life, showing who you are, your future plans and how you spend your time. The catalyst to writing this book was to design a simple budget assisting people to meet their goals. With the No Fail Money Karma Budget Plan we see the issues there are in creating a purposeful existence related directly to the control we have of our finances.

Jonathan noticed a difference between clients who could balance and enjoy life, and those who felt overwhelmed by the daily grind of work and family. The successful clients planned and developed interests and careers they found rewarding, including activities such as sport, community groups, clubs and others. Time management was a major factor in their lives as well as health and exercise. This group also lived within a budget and had their retirement goals organised. In the area of employment, most people in this group had selected and studied for a career they found rewarding. When it

> *An education isn't how much you have committed to memory, or even how much you know. It's being able to differentiate between what you do know and what you don't.*
> – ANATOLE FRANCE

came to purchasing assets, members of this group had a detailed plan including risk assessment, diversification of assets and an understanding of the time frame for the assets to appreciate.

From this assessment we learned that managing your finances successfully had to include all elements within your life, because you cannot separate the management of your money from how you live. The failure to understand this is why many people struggle with the daily demands of work, money management and home life.

Jonathan then studied those people who had little control over their finances and either accumulated high levels of debt or just spent the money they earned with no savings in place and few assets. This group had no budget. They had no plan for the future and used their money to create a lifestyle that they would not be able to maintain in the long term. They did not understand the significance of accumulating assets which would grow in value such as **shares**, well-located property or other investments or they would accumulate assets such as property or shares without having done the necessary research.

> *Real poverty is less a state of income than a state of mind.*
> — GEORGE GILDER

They accumulated consumable goods that would never grow in value, such as cars, stereos and clothes. Often these purchases were made on credit, requiring high interest repayments. Any extra funds the people in this group received would be used to service the debt they accumulated. This group frequently used shopping as a leisure activity, often purchasing unnecessary goods on credit. They worked to pay off high levels of debt and felt they had very little control over their finances. Many were in jobs they found unrewarding but they had seriously limited their options because they needed additional income to maintain their current lifestyle and service their debt level.

From these two groups came the Money Karma Quadrant (page 18), designed to incorporate all elements of our lives. We both learnt from our own experience that enjoying life should include health, exercise, work, friendships, family, money management and leisure. We realised

Money Karma could be achieved by using a variety of worksheets and a budget that required little maintenance once put into place. The key element to successful financial management is developing a process to ensure you meet your goals without spending hours calculating, budgeting and worrying.

Many of us fail to recognise that every cent you spend adds up, and before you know it you can accumulate a vast amount of debt. We both understand how easy it is to lose track of your expenses if you choose to live without a budget. This is why it is essential you take control of your finances.

We supported ourselves through university, working, studying and paying off a mortgage. We really didn't have time to sit down and organise a weekly budgeting session, so we put in place a system ensuring our bills were paid and we had money available for the odd meal out and other activities. We both were raised understanding we had to value money and the effort that went into earning it. The Children's Family Job List Chart (pages 92–3) is based on the one Katherine grew up with. Her grandmother Beula was also very conscious of never spending money without a budget. Beula had a grocery purse where she kept her budgeting shopping money. When sent to the store you would be expected to take the purse and leave the receipt inside with the change so that she could do her accounts. Sometimes Beula would drive 30 miles (48 kilometres) to a grocery store to purchase a particular item, which would save her $1 off the normal price. She drove a Cadillac, which would have consumed more in fuel than the savings she made!

Money Karma has been designed to change the way you manage your finances. When you implement these lessons you can learn how to change your financial destiny forever. Even though there are many finance books on the market today, many people are still facing financial hardship. Many of these guides offer solutions that do not take into account the reader's life experiences. We are all at different stages in our lives and some of us earn more or less than other readers. In *Money Karma* we have factored in these issues so no matter what your experience is, you can begin your journey to financial wellbeing.

We have developed a *Money Karma Lifestyle Planner* CD-ROM which is designed to assist you with organising the financial aspects of your life. You can write to Jonathan Bonnett at Locked Bag 12, Southport 4215 or use the order form on the last page of this book. We wish our readers every success on their journey to attain happiness and financial security.

you, subconsciously. It may consume all that you do and think about. The focus of your life becomes: 'If I had more money I would be happy, because I wouldn't worry about my debts and I could buy whatever I wanted.' Sure, a limitless supply of money would make aspects of our lives easier, but you don't have that limitless supply and the bills are just going to pile up. Even if your money was limitless, happiness is not guaranteed. The reality is that there is more to living than just fulfilling the urge to buy more goods. We're more likely to find contentment by finding balance within our financial and personal lives.

Measuring Happiness

Some of us measure happiness and contentment by what we own and do. When you constantly measure happiness by what you have, or subconsciously believe that you are better than others because you own or earn more than they do, then you are basing your state of happiness on your material wellbeing rather than on humanity. When you base your happiness on materialism, you will never satisfy the need for inner contentment. As soon as you buy the latest computer, there will be another on the market that is more advanced. To stop yourself from spending money and to bring balance back into your life you need to understand that the journey to financial wellbeing begins with self-discipline and **enlightenment**.

Enlightenment

Successful financial planning begins with a journey to enlightenment, that is, an awakening of knowledge and reality. Enlightenment means you are able to have a wider perspective of the world and your place in it. It means you are compassionate, healthy and happy, but most of all you do not allow yourself to be swayed from your ultimate goal of attaining wisdom. It means you are fully aware and understand what you need to do to achieve your full potential as a human being.

Some of us live in a state of semiconsciousness and allow life to continue aimlessly without a plan. For example, you may be in a job that doesn't stimulate your mind, but you convince yourself that it doesn't matter. The money you earn meets all of your living needs, and the thought of change or moving out of your comfort zone seems impossible to achieve. This state can be likened to when we watch TV. You can watch the pictures but may not actively listen to what is being said.

To become more enlightened you learn to be aware of what is happening around you. You make a conscious effort to set goals that will help you focus on creating positive outcomes. This will allow you to start enjoying other pleasures in life. Finding happiness can be as simple as appreciating the joys of a beautiful day, or a wine you've never tasted before. More importantly it is about living in an aware state of mind and experiencing life fully. To live in a conscious state, you have to be aware of how your actions affect the way you live.

The state of your financial affairs is determined by how you live and spend. If you have never evaluated and changed some aspects of your life, it's a fair assumption that you may have difficulty achieving your financial goals. To reach enlightenment means that you start to make decisions for yourself that have positive outcomes and will enable you to develop and grow in the right direction.

Part of the journey towards enlightenment involves creating logical pathways that will help you achieve your financial goals. It's not an easy process and it will take you considerable time to change many of your old financial habits. Always remind yourself that you are embarking on a new course, and if you don't profit from some experiences, you can keep the positive and discard the negative lessons. When you decide you are serious about changing your financial future, you will have to take active steps to stop your old spending and budgeting practices and start something new.

Enlightenment creates a state of contentment and meaning within your life. You will start to care less about possessions. Being enlightened or living in a conscious state can sometimes mean that life has a different purpose. You become aware of the actions you can take and how they affect your quality of life. Everything you do has purpose. The only person who can decide the quality of life you live, or the state of your financial affairs, is you. When you grasp this point and act upon it, you are heading in the right direction. Enlightenment will allow you to achieve a secure financial future.

Self-Discipline

Think of the effort you put into learning to ride a bicycle or drive a car. Recall how much self-discipline you needed to achieve your goal. Managing your finances is similar to riding a bike – you must follow specific steps to succeed. If you try to race down the street before you've learned to balance properly you will fail. Managing your finances is just the same: you cannot go out and buy the Porsche and then work out how you will pay it off.

It will help if you understand that **you** hold all of the answers to successful money management. Start looking at money as an energy force that creates positive and negative effects on your lifestyle. The next time you go out and make an unplanned purchase, consider the effect this purchase will have on your financial wellbeing. If the purchase is going to cause you negative energy when you get your credit card account, then evaluate if it's worth having. Don't allow yourself to create this negative energy. Instead, think of the debt you already have and how relieved you will feel at the end of the month without the extra debt on your credit card account. The relief of not buying unplanned purchases creates a positive energy

> *Delusion means you are not aware of your own fundamental mind; enlightenment means you realise your own fundamental essence. Once enlightened, you do not become deluded any more. If you understand mind and objects, then false conceptions do not arise; when false conceptions do not arise, this is acceptance of the beginninglessness of things. You have always had it, and you have it now. There is no need to cultivate the Way and sit in meditation.*
>
> – ZEN ESSENCE, THE SCIENCE OF FREEDOM, ZEN MASTER MAZU

> *Chains of habit are too light to be felt until they are too heavy to be broken.*
>
> — WARREN BUFFETT

that does not weigh you down with worry. The power of realising your self-control will be reward in itself.

In Jonathan's experience some clients have not understood that self-discipline is a factor preventing them from meeting their financial goals. If you have self-discipline you do not deviate from your desired path. Everything we do in life has a consequence and impacts on our overall wellbeing. The solution to successful financial management includes holistically examining your life, and not separating the financial aspects of your lifestyle.

Several years ago Jonathan met a couple who needed some financial advice because they found they wanted more from their money than they were getting. They wanted him to help them work out a financial plan that would assist them with financial preparation for retirement and the ability to buy their own home.

Trevor and Kelly

Trevor (42) and Kelly (38) are both well educated professionals earning salaries that most of us would dream of having. Kelly is an architect and her partner, Trevor, is a computer software developer. They both enjoy life to its fullest. They have two dependent children who attend private school. Kelly and Trevor both own expensive cars and when Trevor recently made bonus, he upgraded his year-old Mercedes sedan to a Mercedes coupe. Kelly drives a new Porsche, which she's owned for over a year. They dine out on average five nights a week and also have takeaway meals for lunch and at times breakfast on the go. They rent an expensive house in a good neighbourhood and when they moved in, Kelly bought new furniture to match the style of the home. The problem they have is that despite the large salaries they generate, they are accumulating debt in order to maintain their high standard of living.

Each time one of them receives a pay rise, the money is used to purchase new goods. Both Kelly and Trevor are concerned that they don't own a home. They are finding it difficult to save the necessary deposit for the style of home they would like to own.

They wanted Jonathan to devise a plan using tax effective strategies that would not change their lifestyle, but would increase their savings. They believed this would help them to buy a house. The first step in giving financial advice was to make them realise that a financial advisor could not make their money go further. It was for them to decide where to spend their money and where to make cuts in order to reach their goal of saving for a deposit. Jonathan requested that they produce a budget.

At the next session they returned with a completed budget detailing all they spent. It clearly showed they had created their financial situation by allowing themselves to spend money on whatever they desired, without limits. Both needed to understand the difference between needing two cars, and needing two late model European sports cars! Their budget showed there were many opportunities for them to economise, for example, they could reduce the number of takeaway meals they ate and prepare more meals at home. These changes would make a difference to their budget and lifestyle.

This couple unfortunately did not see that they had created a lifestyle they could not sustain. Despite their high incomes they were living beyond their means, but they could not accept this. They could not understand why a certified financial planner could not resolve their financial problem without them having to consider their lifestyle choices. They left dissatisfied that with their combined salary Jonathan could not help them achieve their unrealistic goal. Ultimately, we are each in control of our own life and only we can decide to change the parts of our lives that are causing financial pain.

Throughout our journey to enlightenment it helps to understand the meaning of outward and inner empowerment. Those driven by outward empowerment live their lives based on what others think about them and what they own. For example, a person driven by outward empowerment might only buy designer clothes with logos in an effort to gain status from their clothes, rather than from their own achievement. There is nothing wrong with owning these clothes if you can afford them and you are buying them for your own enjoyment. However, if you are buying them with the thought that it will make people envious of your image, then you are outwardly empowered. Being outwardly empowered can also lead to great debt, because, for example, you may choose to go into debt for new clothes, rather than have others think you are not affluent.

> *Take a method and try it. If it fails, admit it frankly, and try another. But by all means, try something.*
>
> — FRANKLIN ROOSEVELT
> (1882–1945)

To be empowered from within means that you are realistic and content with your situation. With this balance and your finances under control, you understand what will make you happy. Therefore the consequence of making negative or positive decisions both personally and financially gives you a clear understanding of how to live within your means. You don't feel the need to impress friends or relatives with your possessions. You measure your state of happiness differently from an outwardly empowered person, by being grateful for all that you have, and by valuing who you are as an individual. You appreciate your quality of life. There is always going to be someone better off than you, and someone who is not as fortunate. From this you can see how your outlook on life helps determine your personal happiness.

Wish List

This chart is designed to help you identify and explore your dreams and goals. Write down all the things that you wish you could achieve in the first column (for example, a new swimming pool, car or furniture etc.). Be totally honest, as there is no right or wrong answer. No one else will view this list unless you decide to share it.

Goals	Cost	Debt	Why Needed
1 New car (example)	$35000	Debt in one year	Other car 2 yrs old
2			
3			
4			
5			

Goals	Cost	Debt	Why Needed
6			
7			
8			
9			
10			
11			
12			
13			
14			
15			
16			
17			
18			
19			
		TOTAL:	

Once you have listed your goals, estimate the cost of the items in the second column.

In the third column note down a D for Debt if you would have to go and borrow money to meet this cost. Also write down the time frame for the purchase.

Now write down in the final column why you need the listed item.

Total the cost of the items you have listed. You may be surprised by the cost of all the items you've listed as things you would like to achieve.

Go through the list a second time, eliminating items you think you could live without. Look at how much money you have saved yourself.

This short exercise shows you how empowered and in control of your financial destiny you have become. You decide on the debt you are prepared to service. You should also consider the cost of the interest added to the debt. Estimate the years of working you will need to put into servicing these debts.

Is it worth it? Only you can decide.

Money Karma Quadrant

ONE **FINANCE** Debt Living Expenses Future Savings B A L A N C E	TWO **FAMILY – PERSONAL** Quality time, happiness Personal Growth Experiences and memories B A L A N C E
THREE **WORK – CAREER** Education Ambition Time management B A L A N C E	FOUR **LIFESTYLE** Leisure Friendships Exercise and diet B A L A N C E

The purpose of the Money Karma Quadrant is to help you achieve balance in all areas and attain a satisfying quality of life. Some people place too much emphasis on financial issues, due to debt and poor money management habits. This imbalance interferes with the other three broad areas within your life, because you are consumed with the worry of obtaining extra funds to pay your debt. From this scenario, can you see how you consciously choose to neglect other areas within your life? By allowing yourself to be continually consumed with debt issues, you will never achieve inner contentment and happiness. Money Karma is based on balance, and we can create balance because we control our own financial destiny. Ultimately it is all about choice and balance.

Richard

Jonathan had a client who allowed his life to become consumed with debt problems. He was an administrator earning $35,000 p.a., married, with three children all attending primary school. Throughout his working career he had a reputation for getting the job done, on time and often under budget. He was seen as a reliable, well organised worker and this had contributed to his being promoted to a new position earning $45,000 p.a. Everything looked great until he and his wife felt they needed to move into a larger home more befitting his recent promotion into middle management.

*Within months of this move, he became despondent at work with increased absenteeism. Consequently staff morale dropped and the company profits in his area declined. He could no longer focus on his job. His debt problems consumed every aspect of his life. He and his wife had taken on too high a mortgage when they bought their new home and most of Richard's income went to servicing this debt. As well as the increased mortgage repayments they had also bought a new car, contributing further to their debt. Richard suddenly became ill and was off work for two months, without any **INCOME PROTECTION INSURANCE**. Although they financially survived this two-month period, the strain of their debt made life very difficult and unhappy.*

From this family's misfortune we see the need to create harmony or balance within your life. When you have debt problems, you can't enjoy a good quality of life. You have chosen to make a conscious decision to place all of your energy into paying off your debt, leaving no time or attention for leisure, friends or even your job. Your main focus is repayment of debt.

Reassess your Wish List (page 16) and decide whether these items are worth the debt. There is no right or wrong answer. Always consider your quality of life. Every financial decision will have its impact on your lifestyle. Finally, when you have acquired a comfortable level of balance with the way you manage your finances, you will have Money Karma.

Summary

- Your main focus should not be limited to money management and debt reduction.
- Avoid creating financial hardship by over-investing in your present lifestyle.
- Seeking Money Karma will promote the right attitude, self-discipline and priorities for the management of your money.
- We all have a financial fingerprint and no one spends or lives the way we do.
- Avoid one size fits all financial strategies.
- Real happiness is not based on materialism.
- Enlightenment means you are self-aware and you understand what you need to achieve your full potential as a productive human being.
- Set yourself goals, focusing on creating positive outcomes.
- Only you can decide the quality of your life and the state of your financial affairs.
- Don't allow your lack of self-discipline to reduce your chances of meeting your future goals.
- Your subconscious and conscious mind should not be clouded by debt issues, which prevent you from achieving inner contentment and happiness.
- Positive Money Karma is based on balance, and we can create balance because we control our own financial destiny.

The Subconscious Mind and Its Power

*Good and bad come from your own mind. But what do you call your own mind, apart from your actions and thoughts? Where does your mind come from?
If you **really** know where your own mind comes from, boundless obstacles caused by your own actions will be cleared all at once.
After that, all sorts of extraordinary possibilities will come to you without your seeking them.*

— Zen Master Dahui

> *All people desire happiness, and happiness is a result of a healthy state of soul.*
> — Plato (427–347 BC)

The conscious mind comprises an endless, intelligent entity, recreating aspects of our lives and experiences. With this creative force our subconscious mind merges with the conscious mind, enabling us to prioritise those things we consider vital for our sense of comfort and existence.

The mind is an energy force bridging the conscious, which has limitations, to the subconscious, with its inexhaustible boundaries. It is always conceding to conscious or subconscious directions. Everything we think registers in our subconscious mind and subsequently directs our conscious thought.

Make a list of life objectives and start working out what it is you desire from life. There are no rules for success other than believing in yourself. You need to step outside of your comfort zone and experience life. Of course nothing comes without its challenges, and you will find that when you do step outside your comfort zone, you can be affected by either positive or negative experiences. In our opinion it seems irrational to expect to live a life that is only experienced on one level, a level where your daily routine never changes, and your financial situation remains the same.

If you continually tell yourself you are worthless or you will never succeed in life, your life will be determined by these messages. Use only positive messages, which will provide the positive energy force that will compel you to succeed. Your **essence** is the core of your subconscious. This is who you really are, not the image you project when you are at work or out with friends, but your true character and being. Your essence is your dreams, desires and the fun side you may frequently suppress.

When we are young our minds are

> *A minute's success pays the failure of years.*
> — Robert Browning (1812–89)

very susceptible to all the messages we receive. If we were told we are shy, not intelligent, angry, sweet or happy this information is stored in our subconscious mind. As we grow and mature, these messages are still there in our subconscious, and we may act out these characteristics in our every day life.

If we don't like the experiences we have created in our lives, we must first recognise this character trait and actively try to change any aspects of ourselves with which we are unhappy. We all have the energy and power within our mind to alter the negative experiences in our lives. No one but you has the ability to alter your future pathway.

Whatever the past holds you must acknowledge it, but you do not need to waste energy continually reliving life patterns you are dissatisfied with. You must start reprogramming your mind by acknowledging character traits that deter you from achieving your desired destiny. Whatever you subconsciously believe, you will live it out daily, year by year, decade by decade until you take control and change the negative messages and beliefs that are impeding your progress. *Believe in yourself and you will succeed!*

> *Our conscious mind always responds to the power of positive thinking with a positive outcome.*
> – ANONYMOUS

Empower yourself with the realisation that, when making decisions, they may change your life forever. Remember, one left turn instead of one right, and the pathway of your life experience might change forever. Do not be afraid of changing direction if you believe it to be the right decision.

To bring change in your life you may need to step outside your comfort zone, and you may have negative as well as positive experiences. Even though you may be scared of failure, nothing great ever comes to those who fear living. The only factor holding you back from achieving your destiny is fear. Part of living life to its fullest is to take the chance of challenging yourself by continually setting new goals.

Setting Goals

Why is it that some of us can achieve success, while others find the daily tasks of life hard to manage? This is simply because successful people continually create successful thoughts. You are capable of acquiring this inner belief and attaining whatever you desire. Your success can be diminished only if you fail to focus and utilise the positive power of your own thoughts.

> *Our deeds determine us, as much as we determine our deeds.*
> — GEORGE ELIOT
> (1819–80)

Many people have aspirations of achieving a promotion, buying a new house, or starting a fitness schedule. Many fail because they never implement a plan to achieve these goals. People who achieve great success often focus on their desired outcomes and ensure they have a plan to achieve their goal. You must develop a mindset which reaffirms your beliefs and sets these goals into motion.

For example, many of us see ourselves as deserving of a promotion at work. But frequently the reality is that we are not contributing the extra work required. Often, we desire promotion but have a mindset that is still locked on a work schedule of nine to five. You can't achieve your goal if you don't put in extra effort. Look at how well you perform, the effectiveness of ideas or innovations you bring to the organisation, and then assess your worthiness for promotion. Would the company profit from your promotion? This is a difficult exercise, as we often overlook our own inadequacies. We find others to blame for our failure. Take the opportunity now: challenge yourself and start examining your value. There are no rules for success other than believing in yourself.

To reach a goal you need to consciously work towards achieving it. This book will show you ways to take control of your negative emotions and, using the power of your subconscious, to achieve your potential.

Lasting Success is Achievable

In order to achieve your dream or to plan your future destiny, you need to:

- work out exactly what you want to achieve
- design a plan to ensure you achieve your goal.

How many times have you set yourself goals and not achieved any of them? A classic example of this is on New Year's Eve, when everyone sets themselves a resolution. By the second week in January most people have gone back to their old habits and given up the thought of ever attaining their goal. The reason they have failed is that they didn't subconsciously believe they would reach their goal.

Another factor hindering success is that we often allow others to dictate what we can achieve. If you are in debt, and you want to get rid of your debt, you may find you have two barriers stopping you from succeeding. One of these barriers is yourself, as you subconsciously believe you are no good with finances or the high cost of living is causing you to stay in debt. Often there is a second barrier caused by friends or family who reinforce excuses for debt issues. You subconsciously believe the excuses and continue to live with debt. Friends or family may blame debt on the government, banks and globalisation but have failed to identify issues such as over-spending, living without a budget, or simply a lack of self-discipline. What you do today has an effect on how you will live for the rest of your life.

Only those who have changed their mindset will have adopted the strategies they need to succeed. These are the people who will find happiness, because they have taken control. If you ignore what others think or say about you, and only focus on achieving your goal, you will succeed. The only thing holding you back from success is your mind, and that is all you have to change to reach your goal.

Prioritise What is Important

> *Ask a successful busy person to do something for you and they will get it done.*
> — ANONYMOUS

What are your priorities? You may not be succeeding because you are trying to live up to an ideal rather than putting your efforts into a project that will bring you personal satisfaction. You may need to reprioritise what is important and why you are not getting where you want. For example, do you really find it more important to have your house sparkling clean, than to spend more time with your family, friends or enjoying some leisure?

Bob

Bob left school aged 15 and got an apprenticeship as a plumber. By the time he was 26 he was married with three children, had a mortgage and, to his mind, an unchallenging existence. He thought he was capable of more, so he decided to challenge himself and go to university. Bob was intimidated by the prospect of attending a university because he had never seriously believed he was capable of attaining a higher education. His family members voiced their doubt at his choice to return to study. Despite their negative messages he pursued his dream, determined to succeed. He passed his first exams and found that he really enjoyed the opportunity to improve his skills. Bob got a job at a multinational organisation as an administrator and still continued to study part-time. It took Bob seven years to graduate from university because he studied part time and worked full-time. His life started to take a new course and he achieved more than he ever dreamed possible. He is now a well respected and valuable member of his community. In his case, his determination to gain higher education was the key to fulfilling his ideal of success.

Often when we are forced to face our worst fear we are being given the opportunity to challenge ourselves. Had Bob never faced his fear, he would never have achieved his potential. By challenging his subconscious belief that he was not smart enough to attain further education he not only reached his goal, but he used each stage of the process to empower himself. He now has the ability and knowledge to set goals and achieve them.

Do you know what real success feels like? Have you ever forced yourself to take a course or sit an exam? The feeling that comes with passing an exam or succeeding with a challenge we have set ourselves is one of great joy, relief and satisfaction. You seem to develop a greater level of respect for yourself. Once you hit one of your goals, the challenge of taking on the next seems invigorating.

If your goal is to develop an understanding of how to manage you finances and create wealth then you need to set yourself a plan to attain this. All it takes is application, planning and education. You can decide to be one of the few people who challenge themselves to set objectives and succeed in achieving their goals. If you are still faced with money management issues after you've read this book you will need to revisit chapters and challenge yourself again to achieve success.

Motivation for Successful Goal Setting

It is now time for you to examine aspects of your life and determine if you are fulfilling your maximum potential. Are you allowing a subconscious belief to restrict your growth? Have you made a plan of where you want to be in the next five to ten years? Have you even thought about it? If you don't think you need a plan, then you can predict how the next ten years will look. It is as easy as looking at the past ten years; with the only difference being you will look ten years older. However, if you wish to take up the challenge and design your destiny, please fill out the Goal Setting Chart on page 28.

Checklist

- Set your goal.
- Think of how will you start to get there.
- Map each step for each week/day, to achieve the larger goal.
- Visualise each stage as a step on a ladder that you climb up.
- Reward yourself for each success.
- Grow from mistakes.
- Be the best you can be (via education and knowledge).
- Practice a positive mindset.
- Listen to and learn from criticism.

The first stage of this process requires you to identify your goals by writing them down.

Goal Setting Chart

Goal	What You Need to do to Achieve It	Time Frame	Cost	Outcome
Learn how to manage finances and get rid of credit card debt (*EXAMPLE*)	Develop budget, pay of debt, learn and practice new financial management strategies	three years	Total debt to be reduced $40.000 overall	Credit card debt-free able to manage personal finances
University degree (*EXAMPLE*)	Go to uni	three years full-time study or six years part-time	$20,000	University Degree, better prospects and greater self-respect

The second stage of this process requires you to break it down into steps that you must accomplish in the short term to reach your goal.

Stages in Achieving Your Goal

EXAMPLE ONE	
Goal	Learn how to manage finances and get rid of credit card debt
Immediate step	Buy a finance book that you philosophically relate to and examine current spending habits
Stage 2	Read book and collate all financial data
Stage 3	Design an appropriate budget and practice new financial strategies. Plan for debt reduction
Time Frame	One month
Outcomes	Read book. Now understand how to design appropriate budget, adopt new financial strategies, established debt reduction plan
EXAMPLE TWO	
Goal	University Degree
Immediate step	Research universities' courses and enrolment dates
Stage 2	Enrol in course, pay fees and buy texts
Stage 3	Set study pattern and time, management schedule
Time Frame	1st Semester
Outcomes	Passed exam for first unit.

The third part of this process assists you to establish a weekly target. This will ensure that you don't overlook any steps to achieving your goal.

It also assists with time management, as you can use this chart for your entire weekly, monthly and yearly planning. This is just one month; you will need to fill it out for the year to be successful. Break down your goal into daily targets (see charts for Daily Weekly Targets on pages 30–1).

Goal Completion Chart

Weekly Goal	Completed	Due Date	Reward
Read finance book	Yes	Friday	You decide
Complete budget	Yes	Saturday	

It is important that you include leisure as part of your planning process. You should start to introduce activities to help you avoid shopping opportunities if you currently have a debt problem. Shopping as a reward is a tempting way to blow your budget.

If you're trying to eliminate debt as one of your goals, the Money Graph can be a visual stimulant to encourage you to keep on paying off your debt. It is also a reminder of the effort needed to successfully eliminate debt.

You insert the dollar amounts you plan to use to pay off from your salary each week or month and block out each stage as it is achieved.

Money Graph
GOAL: to eliminate $1000 of credit card debt

START   NO DEBT

With this strategy in place, you can now start to consider the positive aspects of how to achieve your goal.

- Focus and consistency are the keys to achieving your goal.
- You must set a plan and stick to it at any cost.
- Don't allow yourself to make excuses.

If you allow yourself to make excuses as to why you need to divert from your new mindset, you are consciously allowing yourself to fail. You will not achieve your goal and you will go back to your old habits. To be the best you can and to achieve your true destiny, you must aim to

Daily & Weekly Targets

This series of charts is designed to help you achieve your goals. When you attain them, reward yourself for persistence and consistency. You should consider using exercise as part of your reward system, as exercise benefits your mind and spirit.

Goal: Manage finances and get rid of credit card debt (example)

	Mon	Tues	Wed	Thurs
WEEK 1	Buy finance book	Read and take notes	Read **PAY DAY**	Read
2	Collate finance data	Calculate all debt; break down into categories	Work out credit card debt strategy	Design liveable financial strategy **PAY DAY**
3	Start living with new budget plan			
4	Make adjustments to new budget			
5				
6				

	Fri	Sat	Sun	Goal Completed
WEEK 1	Read		Leisure activity	Read Book **YES**
2	Organise to open new bank accounts to assist with managing budget	Buy pocket budget book for recording daily expenses	Leisure activity	Designed budget **YES**
3	Pay off first part of credit card debt	A moment of joy – you are taking positive steps towards your goal	Leisure activity	Paid off first payment towards credit card debt
4			Leisure activity	
5				
6				

never falter from your plan. A great example of perseverance is the four-time winner of the Tour de France cycling race, Lance Armstrong, who does not let any circumstance alter his plan to achieve his goal. Armstrong is an Olympic gold-medal cyclist who after several years of competition at elite levels discovered he had testicular cancer. If you examine his story you can see he had many opportunities to find a reason not to succeed in his fight to overcome his illness and compete at world-class level, yet he did not fail or even allow the prospect of failure to become part of his world. Instead he worked through the hard times and was victorious.

> *All work and no play makes Jill a very dull girl.*
> — ANONYMOUS

You are capable of achieving your goal. The only things holding you back may be your lack of motivation, self-assurance, and an effective plan. It doesn't matter where you come from, how rich or poor you are, the secret answer to achieving personal success is determined by your honesty, persistence and consistency.

Never lose sight of your goal, and only adopt actions and decisions that will help you reach your goal.

Inner Conversation

In order to achieve your goals you need to adopt an attitude of thinking only positive thoughts about your capability to succeed. Don't allow your inner voice to cast doubt on your ability to achieve your goal. Do not allow doubt to enter your mind in any circumstance. To be a successful person, always believe in yourself and your ability to succeed.

The power of positive thinking is an important process to consider. Of course we all have moments of self-doubt and allow ourselves a moment of self-pity. However, any blame you attribute to other people or situations is counterproductive. You are the only one who has the power to change your current circumstances. By giving yourself positive messages you are consciously choosing your pathway to success.

Tim

Tim had a relative who was by nature a very negative person. She caused a lot of unnecessary grief to anyone who came near her. This person had a mindset that her children were academically superior to anyone else's children she met. Her unkind words had a constant theme of portraying anyone she met as less intelligent. She consciously chose to create unhappiness in any relationship she had. Tim's memory of his relative, whom he has not seen in over 12 years, is one of disrespect. As an adult her unkind words became meaningless. With maturity he was wise enough to know he was the one who would decide what his capabilities could be. He in fact used his memory of her as an incentive to push himself harder and he achieved his dream of becoming a chemical engineer.

Tim's relative probably doesn't even know or remember how unkind she was. Don't allow others to determine what they believe your destiny should be. Believe in yourself and in your plan, say not 'I cannot', but 'I can'! Focus on your own inner power to drive your belief in yourself. Obstacles in our life can give us strength and be a positive force to motivate us. Overcoming obstacles teaches us important life lessons, remembering everything happens for a reason. Always remember you become what you believe.

> *Believe in yourself and in your dream*
> *Though impossible things may seem.*
> *Some day, somehow you'll get through*
> *To the goal you have in view.*
> *Mountains fall and seas divide*
> *Before the one who in his stride,*
> *Takes a hard road day by day,*
> *Sweeping obstacles away.*
> *Believe in yourself and in your plan.*
> *Say not 'I cannot', but 'I can'.*
> *The prizes of life we fail to win*
> *Because we doubt the power within.*
>
> — ANONYMOUS

Understanding Economic Environments

Part of taking control of your destiny is to be in touch with all the factors that may affect your life. To be aware of your economic environment and how it affects your employment situation, become an active information seeker. Listen to a variety of news programs on radio and TV. Reading different newspapers also broadens your knowledge. The information you glean may be very valuable to you personally. For example, when governments speak of income tax cuts or interest rate cuts, they are trying to stimulate the economy as people don't have extra money to spend and need encouragement to do so. Consumers won't have the extra money for holidays, so if you are employed in the tourism industry, business could be slower. This could also affect businesses that support the tourism industry, including hotels, resorts, cafes, restaurants, airlines, and other related enterprises. Unemployment can be a factor, causing those with mortgages or excessive debt hardship during the economic downturn.

One country can have a domino effect on other economies when there is an economic downturn. For example, if the USA cuts jobs in a certain sector because of decreased consumer spending, then it affects the demand for imports into the USA, which affects the countries who export into the USA. It is important to be an active information seeker so that you have an understanding of world trade and how it affects you.

Unemployment or Loss of Income

Some of us may face the prospect of being unemployed at some time in our working career. The difficult task with being unemployed is designing an appropriate budget to ensure you can maintain a reasonable standard of living. If it should happen to you, the first thing to do is make a detailed list of all of your liabilities and assets. Next you need to modify your lifestyle by cutting out any services or areas within your life you could live without, as these may add excessive costs to your budget. For example, if you regularly get your lawns mowed, house professionally cleaned, dog washed or laundry/dry cleaning, then you need to consider cutting back on these services until you find employment. You should also consider reducing your entertainment costs, such as eating out or going to the movies, etc.

> *It's a recession when your neighbour loses his job; it's a depression when you lose your own.*
> — HARRY S. TRUMAN

If you have the funds to invest a good risk management strategy to protect you against the effects of long-term unemployment is to accumulate a diversified portfolio of investments. You can cash in stocks and bonds at a moment's notice. If you have a portfolio that is primarily invested in real estate or other investments, which take time to sell, you may find yourself facing severe debt or bankruptcy due to lack of **liquidity**. Always look to invest your money wisely and do not limit your portfolio to one asset class.

During a period of unemployment the main priority is to keep your spirit up and remain focused on your search for work. It is also important to let your friends and family know of your employment situation as they may know someone who could assist you with finding a job.

Summary

- Everything we think registers within the subconscious mind and subsequently directs our conscious thought.
- There are no rules for success other than believing in yourself.
- When you step out of your comfort zone you will be affected by positive and negative experiences.
- Avoiding challenges is not realistic.
- Nothing successful comes to those who fear life and its challenges.
- Facing your worst fear often gives you the opportunity you need to challenge yourself.
- We create our own experiences and we are responsible for our triumphs and failures.
- Only you have the ability to alter your future pathway.
- Empower yourself with the realisation when making decisions that these may change your life forever.
- Successful people continually embrace successful thoughts.
- Plan to ensure you meet your goals.
- What you do today has an effect on how you will live for the rest of your life.
- Relish feelings of achievement.
- Positive messages lead to positive outcomes.
- Don't allow others to determine your destiny.

3

Budgeting

*Too many people spend money **they** haven't earned, to buy things they don't want, to impress people they don't like.*

— Will Rogers (1880–1935)

> *Resolve not to be poor: whatever you have, spend less. Poverty is a great enemy to human happiness; it certainly destroys liberty, and it makes some virtues impracticable and others extremely difficult.*
>
> – SAMUEL JOHNSON
> (1709–84)

For many people, budgeting is the most difficult habit to acquire. The process of analysing your expenses and being aware of what you spend your money on is crucial to positive Money Karma. Creating a budget you can live with will require some soul searching.

Planning a Budget

The key to developing a successful budget is to establish a cash flow system that helps you meet your goals.

First, find out where your money goes. This may sound rather obvious, but most people don't know where they spend their money. It is not unusual for Jonathan to see clients who cannot account annually for up to $20,000 of after-tax income. They usually don't believe it at first, until you point out that it is $55 per day, and can be caused by all sorts of unplanned purchases including the following typical money expenditure.

Where the Money Goes

Spent On	Cost	Cost per Year
Magazine subscriptions	Average magazine is approx. $5.00 x two per week x one year (52 weeks) ($5x2x52=)	$520.00
Electronic equipment TV sets, video recorders, radios, CD players, kitchen appliances, etc many of these items are never used?	Average TV cost $500–600 kitchen appliances $100 each and radios $20–100.	$1400.00
Mobile phones	Average mobile phone cost plus weekly calls of $20.00 multiplied by two phones in household	$2080.00 + cost of phone

BUDGETING

Spent On	Cost	Cost per Year
Video rental plus late fees	One video per week plus cost of two late days on average – $15.00	$780.00
Buying lunch (sandwich) instead of making it	$5.00 per day, five days a week over the year for one person	$1300.00
Buying a cup of coffee	One cup, five times a week at a cost of $3.50 each ($3.50 x 5 x 52=)	$910.00
Unplanned clothing purchases	(going to shopping malls at lunchtime). On average $30.00 per week over a year. ($30 x 52=)	$1560.00
Take away food	Two nights a week for a family of four, average cost $80.00 per week. ($80 x 52=)	$4160.00
Credit card debt	$1000 on your credit card for one year at 16% interest rate costs – (1000 x 0.16 =)	$160.00
Random gift buying	Average $20.00 per week over a year – ($20 x 52=)	$1040.00
Going to movies	Two adults average $12 per ticket, plus treats $5 per week over a year – ($12 + 5 x 52=)	$1768.00
Manicure/pedicure/massage	One manicure per week average $45, over a year – (25 x 52=)	$2340.00
Wasted food (food you throw away)	Average wastage a week $30 over a year – (30 x 52)	$1560.00
Shoes	Average two pairs never worn cost $100 per pair 2 x $100=	$200.00
Unwanted new clothes	You buy them and then get them home to discover you don't like them, **TAKE THEM BACK**	You can estimate loss if kept and never worn.
CDs	Buy one a week, average cost $10 – $30 over a year $520 up to	$1560.00 per year
Gambling lottery ticket	One ticket a week $5 over a year ($5 x 52)	$260.00
	TOTAL:	

These expenditures total over $20,000, remembering that this is after-tax money. If your household pays an average of 30 per cent in income tax then you need to earn more than $28,000 to collect $20,000.

The listed items give you an idea of how easy it is to spend money without being aware of where all your money goes. Draw up your own list. Remember you are trying to identify where your money is being spent so you need to think about your lifestyle and list the costs.

Expenditure List

Spent On	Cost	Cost Per Year
	Total:	

Once you have completed this chart, add up the total to find your annual cost per year.

This chart gives you an indication of how much money you are really spending. Making yourself aware of this expenditure can help you to change the negative habits of your poor money management. The aim is to create balance, generating positive Money Karma.

One example of how we allow ourselves to spend money we have not budgeted for is over the Christmas holiday period. We allow ourselves to accumulate debt for gifts many of our friends and relatives can live without. We should focus instead on offering gifts from the heart that have a deeper meaning and do not create serious debt. Try recalling the gifts you gave and the gifts you received last Christmas. Then try remembering experiences in your life you really enjoyed. Which mean the most to you?

No Fail Money Karma Budget Plan

This budget requires you to collate information about all your fixed expenses and to assemble the bills into a neat pile. These bills should include your water rates, land rates, housing insurance, car insurance, car registration, mortgage payments, car payments, grocery bills, electricity, gas, cable TV, holiday plans, necessary white good purchase, medical insurance, life insurance, entertainment, credit card bills, clothing, shoes, personal care (hair cuts, pedicures, manicures, massage, gym subscriptions, personal trainer etc.), pet care (dog wash bills, grooming, kennel care, dog registration and vet bills), school/education expenses, dry cleaning, dining out, takeaway food, rent and any other regular bills/debts you accumulate throughout the year.

Separate your bills into two piles. One pile should hold all of the annual expenses and the other pile, your daily living expenses.

> *Success is not final, failure is not fatal: it is the courage to continue that counts. The farther back you can look, the farther forward you are likely to see. The price of greatness is responsibility.*
>
> – SIR WINSTON CHURCHILL (1874–1965)

Pile One	Pile Two
Car registration	Weekly groceries
Car repayments	Weekly alcohol bills
Car servicing	Entertainment including –
Car insurance	takeaway, dining out meals,
House/rent payments	coffees, drinks/snacks while
Housing insurance	out or at work, movies, plays,
Housing rates, water, sewerage	golf, table tennis, squash etc.
Holiday/rental property costs	costs, gambling, lottery tickets,
Christmas fund for gifts	horse racing or dog betting,
Holiday fund	magazine subscriptions or
Emergency whitegoods	purchases, newspapers, video
purchase	or DVD hire or purchases,
Cable TV costs	music purchases, computer
School/education fees	games, Internet downloads,
Savings	lunches bought, breakfasts
Charity	bought, books bought, sweets,
Gardening maintenance	bakery goods, etc.
Credit card debt	Childcare, baby-sitting
Telephone bills including	Transportation – taxi, train,
household and mobile	plane, bus or other
Electricity bills	Hair care colouring, cuts
Gas bills	Dry-cleaning
Health insurance	Clothes, shoes
Personal loans/ debt payments	
Housekeeper (Cleaner)	
Pool cleaner	
Child support payments if divorced	
Superannuation, life insurance or share portfolio purchases.	

Annual Fixed Expenses Table

Bill	Amount	Due Date	Total per Year cost	Divide by 22 (or 11) (see below)	Deduction from fortnightly (or monthly) wage
Car registration					
Car insurance					
Car servicing					
Car other					
House insurance					
House rates, water, sewerage					
Land tax					
Electricity					
Gas					
Pool cleaner					
Gardener/maintenance					
Holiday/rental property bills					
Telephone bills (house)					
Mobile phone bills					
Cable TV					
Emergency white goods purchase					
Christmas gifts fund					
Holiday fund					
Savings					
Charitable donations					
School/education					
Child support payments					
Credit card payment					

Bill	Amount	Due Date	Total per Year cost	Divide by 22 (or 11) (see p. 45)	Deduction from fortnightly (or monthly) wage
Personal or other debt payments					
Cleaner					
Superannuation, (retirement funds) personal insurance or other saving plan					
Health insurance					
Other					
				Total:	

Investment Property Annual Expenses Table

Bill	Amount	Due Date	Total per Year cost	Divide by 22 (or 11) (see p. 45)	Deduction from fortnightly (or monthly) income
Investment property (fixed expenses)					
Rates (land & water)					
Body corporate (if applicable)					
Insurances (building and/or contents – if furnished)					
Interest costs					
Tax accountant					
General maintenance					
Renovating budget					
Bathroom(s)					
Kitchen					
Appliances					

Bill	Amount	Due Date	Total per Year cost	Divide by 22 (or 11) (see below)	Deduction from fortnightly (or monthly) income
Hot water system					
Lounge/Dining					
Laundry					
Carpets/floor coverings					
Painting					
Window coverings (curtains etc)					
Garage					
Driveway paving					
Guttering					
Gardening					
Emergency fund					
Miscellaneous					
				Total:	

To determine how much of your income should be allocated to meet your normal expenses it is necessary to go through this process of examining exactly where your money goes. Then add it up to a yearly total and divide it by 22 if you get paid fortnightly, or 11 if you get paid monthly. This will give you an amount that should be set aside for your living expenses and even includes an inflation factor to ensure that your allocation keeps up with price increases. This amount is automatically deposited into your annual expenditure bank account. For further information see the following section on establishing a cash flow system that will empower you.

Daily Expenses Table

Bill	Amount	Due Date	Total per Year cost	Divide by 22 (or 11) (see p. 48)	Deduction from fortnightly (or monthly) wage
Weekly Grocery					
Weekly Alcohol					
Cigarettes/Cigars					
Day care					
Baby sitting					
Other					
Other					
Transport Toll gates					
Car parking					
Petrol					
Bus, plane, taxi, train other					
Other					
Dry cleaning					
Car/motorcycle payment/s					
Boat payments					
Furniture/electrical hire/purchase					
Other					
Personal hygiene Hair care					
Make-up					
Beauty treatments (manicure/pedicure)					
Other					
Sport Massage					
Gym membership					

BUDGETING 47

Bill	Amount	Due Date	Total per Year cost	Divide by 22 (or 11) (see p. 48)	Deduction from fortnightly (or monthly) wage
Weekly sport (tennis, squash, golf etc)					
Clothes/shoes					
Other					
Entertainment including: Take-away, dining out meals					
Lunches bought					
Breakfasts bought					
Sweets					
Bakery goods					
Coffees, drinks					
Snacks					
Movies					
Plays,					
Gambling, lottery tickets,					
Horse racing or dog betting,					
Book, magazines, subscriptions					
Newspapers					
Video or DVD hire or purchases					
Music purchases					
Computer games					
Internet access					
Other					
				Total	

To determine how much of your income should be allocated to meet your normal daily expenses it is necessary to go through this process of examining exactly where your money goes. What you then need to do is to add it up to a yearly total and then divide it by 22 if you get paid fortnightly, or 11 if you get paid monthly. This will give you an amount that should be set aside for your daily living expenses and even includes an inflation factor to ensure that your allocation keeps up with price increases. This amount is automatically deposited into your daily expenses bank account.

Establish a Cash Flow System that will Empower You

Once you've decided where to spend your money, you will need to open two bank accounts – cheque or savings – with Internet access if you so desire, to manage your daily and annual expenses.

Payments for your annual expenses are to be automatically deposited into the account that caters for these expenses. This account should, if possible, be opened with a $500 float to ensure that any large bills don't empty the account in the first few months. It is never to be used for any other purpose. Be realistic with your budget allocation. The system set out allows a 10 per cent safety buffer so there is no reason to inflate your amounts. In the first year you will find you need to adjust your expenditure. You may not have allocated enough money into some sections. By the second year you will have control over your spending so there should be no need to make any further adjustments. Note that the budgeting system has already factored in inflation.

This process takes some establishing and may end up costing you extra in bank fees. However using these bank accounts will make managing your money more efficient, make you more productive, and allow you to enjoy life more.

If you traditionally use credit cards to pay your bills and you have the control to pay off the credit limit, then there are options available to you using your credit card. Remember it is important you only use two credit cards.

BUDGETING

First, organise a **charge card** for your fixed daily expenses. A charge card is one that must be paid off in full at the end of every month. There is no limit on a charge card so you need to be very careful of how you use this card. We suggest you only spend what you can afford to pay off. These cards are helpful as they force you to control your spending.

> *The truth shall make you free.*
> — JOHN 8:32

You should now obtain a second card, this time a credit card that you can use when the charge card will not be accepted. Apply the same principle to the credit card as to the charge card, paying the balance off in full when you receive the bill.

Using your newly acquired charge card and using your daily fixed expenses bank account, deposit all the cash your budget requires for your food and other daily purchases that you will use to pay with the charge card. This means that every pay period you may have allocated, for example, $300 a week for food. So you deposit this $300 from your wage into your charge card account. Thereby you have already paid for the goods and there is no excess money in your account, tempting you to spend wastefully. This means your bills are always paid on time. *Beware* when deciding whether to obtain a charge card, because there is no limit as to how much you can spend each month. If this may be a problem for you then you need to get a credit card with a specific limit but for this system to work you must use the same principles as a charge card and pay off the entire credit card bill at the end of every month. Remember your goal is to have a budgeting system you control and that does not allow you to accumulate bad debt which costs you more in interest charges. Bad debt also stops you from meeting goals you have planned for.

This strategy is also useful if you are going on holiday.

- Deposit all of your spending money into the account and you will not have a bill when you return from your trip. Beware not to spend more than you have allocated for each area of your holiday budget. The charge card strategy is useful as it limits the cash you carry and the temptation of spending on unplanned purchases.

After this exercise, many of Jonathan's clients find that they have paid off their debt and have extra money. Take our advice, don't be scared to save. Ideally, you should aim to have between $1000 and $3000 saved as a safety net. You never know when you may be faced with an emergency and need money, for example, to visit a sick relative, or repair your home after a severe storm. While you are reducing your debt you may wish to keep a credit card with a limit of $5000 as a substitute for emergency cash. The usual cautions should apply in that it must only be used for emergencies.

If you can adopt these strategies you will find that you are no longer accumulating debt, but rather finding new opportunities to explore life. You will be inclined to spend less time window-shopping and making unplanned purchases. Only go shopping for planned purchases. If you feel your only enjoyment in life is spending or going shopping and accumulating debt, you need to take a look at your inner self. Always remember, life is what you choose to make of it.

Successful money management is not about diminishing your lifestyle. Don't reduce the quality of your life to a level of misery simply to pay your mortgage off in one year. Taking control means spending within your means and having a balanced plan that fits in with your life. Successful money management is about balance: in the same way that a good diet should not involve living on avocados and lemons for months at a time, but enjoying different foods in moderation.

Accounting for Your Money

Having completed your budget charts, it is time to decide if you like what you have learned about yourself and your spending habits. You may have realised you were spending more money each month than you were bringing in. You have created an opportunity for empowerment in deciding where cutbacks are to be made. It helps if you look on this stage as a learning process. The positive karma to this process allows you to learn and grow from this experience. You may even feel a sense of relief at having discovered your financial habits were not healthy or sustainable. You now have the chance to take steps to improve the way you currently manage your money.

If you find you have completed this process and are feeling angry or upset by learning what your real financial situation is then try to think positively! By completing the tables above you have taken the first step to becoming a financially secure person. If you allow yourself to wallow in self-pity about your financial situation you will never get out of it. Remember the saying 'No pain no gain?' Well, once you have felt the pain you are on your way to becoming a financially secure person. If you choose to do nothing after learning about your current financial state, then you have no one but yourself to blame for a financial life filled with juggling bills and living from pay to pay without any cash reserves. If you have read this far without filling out your budget, now is the time!

Deciding Where to Spend It

Start this section by investing in a pocket notebook that you carry with you always. Every time you spend money, record it in your pocket book. Whenever Jonathan's clients undertake this exercise, they begin to see where all of their money has been spent. Later many tell him how shocked they were at the vast amounts of money they spent without realising.

As a quick exercise work out your annual after-tax income. For example, say you earn $30,000. Subtract the tax, which would be $5380. This would leave you with $24,620. Now take this figure and divide it by 365 days. The amount you are left with is how much you earn in one day: $67.45. Using your pocket book as a guide see how many times in a week you would spend more than you earn on any given day. As easy as it is to spend more than the $67 a day you need to remember that you have not yet deducted your daily living costs from the $67. If your rent is $300 a week it costs $42 a day just to pay for the roof over your head. Your $67 a day is now down to $25 a day. Now that $25 must pay for your food, electricity, etc. Is it any wonder that we find ourselves living with a budget that cannot be sustained?

$30,000 (gross income) − $5380 (tax) = $24,620 (net income)
$24,620 divided by 365 = $67.45 per day

Reviewing Your Budget

Review the budget charts you completed earlier. You need to calculate if you are living beyond your means. If your budget charts reflect that you are spending more than you earn, then you need to decide where to cut back. You need to understand the concept of needs versus wants (refer to Chapter 4, Debt Wisdom), and if you do so then making cuts to your budget should not be too difficult an exercise. If you can master this aspect of your life, you will be rewarded with a quality of life free from negative Money Karma, which creates stress and debt. Don't spend more than you earn, and to help monitor this, always keep a pocket book recording your daily spending habits.

Everyone should have a discretionary spending amount to be spent how they wish. Apportion a discretionary spending amount of, for example, $20 to $30 per week. If you are in a relationship, one partner should not criticise the other for 'wasting' these funds. This is their 'freedom money', and we all need to have some.

The budget charts will help you decide where to spend your money. The fixed expenses account cannot be diminished for any reason, but the daily expenses account allows you to make positive decisions.

If you have successfully made it through to the end of this chapter and you have completed the budget exercise, you have taken control of your financial destiny. Congratulations – this means you are on the pathway out of debt and in step with the joys a debt-free life has to offer.

Summary

- Gather the facts, finding out where your salary is spent each pay period. If you have never produced a personal budget and have no idea of how to start, we suggest you consider the No Fail Money Karma Budget Plan.
- The key to establishing a successful budget is to create a cash flow system that enables you to meet your goals.
- Know where you spend your money.
- Carry a pocket book for recording your daily expenditure.
- Ensure you know how much money you earn each day and whether you spend more than you earn.
- Practise the self-discipline of maintaining a budget.

4

Debt Wisdom

*Rarely do we find men who **willingly engage** in hard, solid thinking. There is an almost universal quest for easy answers and half-baked solutions. Nothing pains some people more than having to think.*

— Martin Luther King Jr (1929–68)

Ultimately we'd all like to achieve freedom from debt. **Debt wisdom** is about more than just balancing the bankbook; it is about being prepared for any unforeseen events in your life that may impact on your personal and financial wellbeing. Debt wisdom is having a holistic approach to life, recognising actions and behaviour that create money management issues. It is the process of understanding the difference between **good debt** and **bad debt** and how easy it is to make the wrong financial decision.

> *We can loan you enough money to get you completely out of debt.*
> — Undisclosed Financial Institution

Too often, we repeat our negative actions without making a conscious effort to change. Debt wisdom serves the positive purpose of preventing us from reacting negatively to profound events (such as the death of a partner, divorce, the birth of a child, or making a poor investment decision) and their long-term consequences and implications. These events can impact upon our finances as we make drastic or poor decisions with our money to cope with these incidents. You can achieve the ultimate goal of attaining debt wisdom, leading to financial planning and freedom from debt.

To appreciate the lessons of debt wisdom you need to gain a deeper awareness of the actions and thoughts caused by happenings around you, both global and local. This chapter will help you adopt some useful strategies that will limit your spending on items you don't need. You will begin to see how easy it is to allow negative Money Karma into your life, by ignoring the basic concept of self-discipline.

> *It is better to have a permanent income than to be fascinating.*
> — Oscar Wilde (1854–1900)

To live a life based on the principle of self-discipline, you need to understand the difference between controlling your own destiny and good luck.

Controlling your destiny means you have studied and planned the way you manage your life. You leave nothing to chance, because you have goals and the self-discipline to achieve them. When you elect to live a life based on good luck, it means you have no plan or goals, and leave your dreams to chance. Don't place yourself in a position where your only financial strategy is based on good luck, such as winning the lottery. You need to have a constructive plan to follow to achieve your ultimate goal, leading to financial independence.

> *The truth of the matter is you always know the right thing to do. The hard part is doing it.*
>
> — GENERAL NORMAN SCHWARZKOPF

The negative energy that consumes our lives when we have high levels of debt is the most common cause of relationship breakdown. It is devastating to see relationships deteriorate because of money issues. We frequently allow ourselves to spend money we don't have. Why are so many of us unable to recognise that we are living beyond our means? It is usually because we lack clearly defined goals and the self-discipline to make decisions about what we need and don't need. Negative Money Karma can seriously affect our health.

You can stop spending money you don't have. Focus on creating your own destiny. It begins with deciding what you want to achieve. If you have consumer debt (credit cards, personal loans, store cards etc.) then getting rid of this debt should be your number one goal. What you must do is decide what to spend your money on. This sounds like an easy concept, yet so many of us don't understand the difference between a need and a want. Begin by reviewing your current spending habits and consciously choosing how you are going to spend your money.

Needs Versus Wants

Let's examine this concept in depth. Some of you may have heard about Abraham Maslow's hierarchy of needs. Maslow was a psychologist who developed a theory based on needs. He believed that having achieved each stage of the 'needs process', you move onto the next stage.

In a hierarchy of needs, the first stage relates to basic needs such as food, water, shelter and transportation to and from work. The second stage consists of security needs. People need to feel secure in their jobs, safe in their homes, and confident about their retirement. At the third stage are 'belonging' needs. People seek association with others. The forth stage is 'Love' – humans need to be wanted and loved, fulfilling the desire for self-esteem. The fifth stage and highest level of Maslow's hierarchy of needs are self-actualisation needs. Once the first four needs are met, Maslow says, people are free to achieve maximum personal potential, for example, by travelling extensively or perhaps becoming an expert on great Australian and New Zealand wines.

From this description, you will recognise that a need is something that you must have to survive, for example food, shelter, security etc. A want is something that does not make a difference to your survival, like a new CD, a new car or a swimming pool.

This is one of the hardest concepts to grasp because we often allow ourselves to believe that without purchasing that new CD, we are missing out on a need. If your credit cards are at their maximum and you have no savings, then this purchase is a want and not a need. Another way to assess a need versus want is to think about the money you currently have in savings (if any) and the amount of money owed on all your credit cards. If you cannot afford to pay off your credit card debt today, then you should not even consider buying anything that is not a need.

One of the greatest myths of the need versus want theory is that it is the expensive items you purchase which destroy your finances. The reality is the items you buy which seem to cost very little often add up to large sums.

Can you relate to any of the following:

- Does your addiction to credit card spending affect your life?
- Do you find that your income is mainly spent on paying off your mortgage?
- Is your only leisure activity shopping or spending money on items you don't need?
- Are you constantly transferring money from one account to another?
- Do you feel you are a bad parent if your children can't purchase everything they want?
- Do you have goals that you never seem to achieve?
- Does your life revolve around paying off debt instead of enjoying life?
- Are you a problem gambler and in denial?
- Is renting instead of owning your own home a concern for you?
- Are you concerned about saving for your retirement?

You'll deduce from these questions that possessions do not bring happiness. The person who gets the most happiness from you buying a smart new sports car is the salesperson. If you have debt problems, you get five years of finance repayments in which to consider the appropriateness of your purchase.

Money Depression

When you have money problems it can infiltrate every aspect of your life. Sometimes you may feel so overwhelmed by your debt you are suffering from **money depression** and look to blame your situation on other factors.

The symptoms of money depression come in many forms. Some people start to believe that if they had selected a different partner or made other choices in their life, then they would not have their current level of debt, which seems to be destroying their life. The unfortunate part of this dilemma is that we all have choices in life and we are the ones who choose what level of debt we have.

Money depression means you lose the sense of who you are and what your true goals may be. It also means that because of the debts you have accumulated you have chained yourself to your job and most of all you are now chained to the life you have created for yourself. This may not be the life you had dreamed of, but unfortunately it is the life you now own. Getting out of this cycle of debt and starting to live the life you always dreamed of is not as hard to achieve as you believe. The only factor stopping you is yourself, and your choices.

The Money Juggler

A **money juggler** is a person who spends more than they earn and constantly moves money from credit card accounts and bank accounts to pay their bills. Even worse, they pay off one credit card with a cash advance from another card. Do these sound like habits you have adopted in an effort to cover your debts? Well, the simple fact is that at the end of the day you don't have any more money, you have less. You need to get organised and make sure the money you need is available to pay off the monthly bills on time.

Carl

Carl was a money juggler. No matter what he did, he still had the same problem at the end of every month, more outgoings than incomings. Then one day he came over to my house, and told me about a great bottle of champagne he had opened with friends the night before at a dinner party.

The champagne he had consumed was a $400 bottle. Impressed with the quality of this wine he had called all over town looking to purchase a few more bottles. He tracked down four bottles and paid $1600 for the privilege.

What stunned me most was that this person was always the first to complain about the high cost of living, and how he could barely make ends meet on $80,000 a year. He was a bachelor with no dependants or assets.

This story highlights the priorities different people place on different things. Do you see how the choices you make with money influence how much you have to spend on bills and lifestyle? With Carl's high annual income, he should have easily been able to enjoy a good lifestyle and not accrue debt. However, because he felt he had to gratify his extravagant wishes, he was struggling to meet his bills. To some people having an annual income of $100,000 a year is not enough because the repayments on the Porsche and the repayments on the house in a good suburb cost a lot to service. With that income comes the illusion that you can buy expensive meals for dinner every night of the week. It may also mean that you think you can go out and buy designer clothes and spend on other items. Someone else on an income of $40,000 a year may manage to save some money each week, enjoy the odd meal out and even move some funds into different investment alternatives.

To think of it in another context, how many people have you heard say 'If only I was on $200,000 a year all my problems would be over'. They then go on to tell you how they would buy a holiday house, travel the world, buy new furniture, etc. The point is that they would still have the same money problems that they had on a lower income, only they would have a higher debt to pay.

Creating positive Money Karma is about making educated assumptions and allocating your wage into strategic spending patterns. It is about not just spending for the sake of accumulating more debt. Once you understand the 'needs versus wants' concept, you cannot blame anyone other than yourself for unplanned spending.

> *No matter how far you have gone on the wrong road, turn back.*
> – TURKISH PROVERB

> *Take your life in your own hands and what happens? A terrible thing: no one to blame. Advice is what we ask for when we know the answer but we wish we didn't. And the trouble is, if you don't risk anything, you risk even more.*
> – ERICA JONG

Living in a conscious state of mind means you are accountable for all of your actions. Living with positive Money Karma, you know what will make you happy.

Too Much Debt

> *Home life ceases to be free and beautiful as soon as it is founded on borrowing and debt.*
>
> — HENRIK IBSEN

If you have excessive debt and may be considering bankruptcy, there are options for you before you take this step. The first point to think about is that you are a valuable person who has made some mistakes. There is always a solution to every problem. What you need to do is to seek expert professional help earlier rather than later. As a Financial Adviser, Jonathan has dealt with people with serious financial problems seeking professional advice too late to avoid bankruptcy.

When deciding how you will manage and maintain some level of debt within your budget, first consider that all of your expenses, including food, electricity, mortgage, rent etc. should never exceed 70 per cent of your income. This gives you the opportunity to reduce debt and start to build wealth. The largest debt most people will carry is their home loan and possibly a car debt.

Credit Cards and Debt

Most of us believe that if we can afford to pay off the minimum credit card repayment each month and manage to pay for a roof over our heads, then we do not have a debt problem. You need to reassess this situation. You never know how close you could be to bankruptcy.

If a single person or married couple lost their jobs tomorrow, would they be able to cover all of their monthly expenses? If the answer is no, how much money do you have in savings or in investments that could be liquidated to cover living expenses? This is a daunting thought. Every pay is crucial for your financial survival. Should you lose your job and income, how long would it be before the bank and other creditors took legal action against you?

A starting point is to examine all of your credit cards and (**EFTPOS**) **cash cards**. Document how much credit limit, interest rate and balance you have owing on each card. No one can estimate these figures because we really have no idea how much we are paying off until we see the bill each month. Remember, these are just the credit cards we use. Many of us may also have furniture, electrical appliances and other items we pay off on a monthly basis.

Shown below are a sample debt chart as well as a debt chart that you will need to fill out accurately in order to help you eliminate your debts.

Sample Credit Card Debt Chart

Card Name	Card Limit ($)	Interest Rate (%)	Min Repayment ($)	Balance Owing ($)
Visa (example)	3,000	16.9	60	2,900
MasterCard	5,000	16.9	65	3,100
American Express credit	2,000	13.95	30	800

Your Credit Card Debt Chart

Card Name	Card Limit ($)	Interest Rate (%)	Min Repayment ($)	Balance Owing ($)
Visa				
MasterCard				
American Express credit				

Now that you have completed this chart, it is time to devise a plan to assist you to pay off your debt in a strategic manner. First, examine the minimum monthly repayment, as this amount forms part of your fixed monthly expenditure and needs to be paid every month.

The second part of this process is to look at the rate of interest on each of the cards or debts you have detailed. The card with the highest rate of interest is the one you should aim to pay off first. For example, if you have a credit card with an interest rate of 17 per cent and another with a rate of 12 per cent then you need to start paying off the card with 17 per cent interest rate first. If you have spare credit on the lower interest rate card, you can transfer debt from the higher rate card to the lower rate card.

Working out where the extra money will come from to pay off these debts should not be a difficult task if you have completed your budget. Trying to pay off debts without a budget is like going out and buying a Ferrari and then trying to work out how you will pay it off without a plan. The key to success is clearly defined goals and self-discipline. If you have not done your budget yet, turn back to Chapter 3, Budgeting and follow the guidelines there. Without a budget you will never get out of your financial dilemma.

With your budget plan completed, you will know where to find the extra money to pay off debt. Allocate more than the minimum payment to clear these charges, otherwise you will just maintain the same debt level and never get rid of the excess debt.

Here's an example:

Card Name	Card Limit ($)	Interest Rate	Balance Owing ment ($)	Min Repay-debt	Time to pay off years	Total Cost
Visa	3,000	15.25%	2,800	$55	7 years	$4,565

Now observe what happens when you pay an extra $10 a month off the debt.

Card Name	Card Limit ($)	Interest Rate	Balance Owing ment ($)	Min Repay-debt	Time to pay off years	Total Cost
Visa	3,000	15.25%	$2,800	$65.00	5.25 yrs	$4,095

The total saving for the card owner is $470 and nearly two years just for $10 a month extra.

If you make it an extra $100 a month the amount you will save is astronomical:

Card Name	Card Limit ($)	Interest Rate	Balance Owing ment ($)	Min Repay-debt	Time to pay off years	Total Cost
Visa	3,000	15.25%	$2,800	$155.00	1.75 yrs	$3,255

Your saving is $1310 and more than five years, for just $100 a month extra. If this is possible it will make a major impact on your level of financial comfort. The key issue is not to try paying your card off too quickly, leaving yourself short in other areas. Remember: always pay off high interest rate debt first, until eliminated.

The next strategy is designed to ensure that you do not accumulate more debt, having cleared this debt from your credit cards. We suggest you destroy each card as you pay it off, and limit yourself to holding only two cards at any time (see Chapter 3, Budgeting for more detail). One should be a charge card, which means that it must be paid off by the end of the month. The other is to be used just for the times the charge card is not accepted by some establishments. This ensures that you do not allow yourself to acquire unnecessary debt by being tempted to make unplanned purchases. Remember: deposit your daily expenses amount into your charge card account. If you use the charge card to buy planned goods such as clothing, make-up, etc. you must deposit this allocated money into the charge card account each pay period.

Managing Your Credit Card Debt

Consider the three options listed below.

1. Every month deposit your entertainment and clothing allowance into your charge or credit card account. This way you have already paid for the items you are going to buy. Always know your limit.
2. Take all of your credit cards out of your wallet and store them in a secure place. This will mean that when you are out shopping you cannot make unplanned purchases. If this should fail, destroy your credit cards.
3. Only take your credit cards with you for planned purchases. Take a notebook

when you go shopping and write down all of the prices and items you would have purchased if you had your credit cards with you. When you get home review your list and total the cost. Now add on the interest of the credit card and give yourself six months to pay off the goods. Chances are you will be pleased that you didn't waste more money on credit card debt than you could afford.

These strategies will ensure that you only spend money you have allocated in your budget. It also means that you will not be tempted to acquire new unplanned purchases.

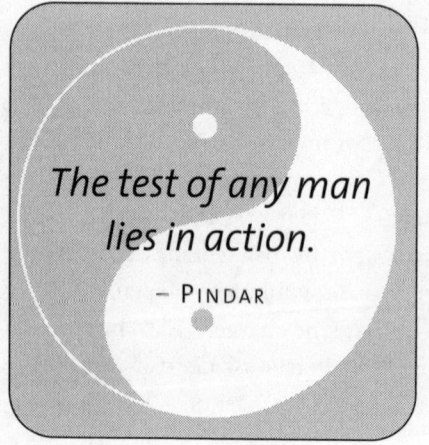

The test of any man lies in action.

— PINDAR

Taking control of your finances also means that you do not allow your bank or building society to increase your credit limit. Periodically they will send out letters inviting you to increase your limit. Throw them away immediately, and don't ever allow the bank or building society to take control of your financial destiny as this creates bad Money Karma.

Develop positive patterns to control your debt. Take one day at a time, and set yourself realistic goals. If you have a series of credit cards loaded to the maximum limit, then you need to organise yourself to take control of this challenge. Start by setting yourself the goal of paying one card off. Once you have achieved this goal you will find this motivates you to pay off the rest. You will feel empowered and liberated from a burden that was destroying your life. Once you have done this, you realise that you are in control of your financial destiny. The restoration of balance in your life will be a reward in itself.

If you get caught in a cycle of debt, go and talk to your creditors. Use all the help offered to find a positive outcome. Maintain a positive attitude: evaluate your present situation and do the very best to meet your responsibilities with integrity.

Good Debt and Bad Debt

Is there such a thing as good debt? This will be a concept many of you may not have heard of. Some debt can actually assist you in achieving goals. Investors often use borrowed funds geared to invest in assets, which they believe will return a greater rate of return than the interest paid. This type of debt is classified as good debt, because you are investing borrowed money into income producing assets. Investing in this way is not without risk. Careful assessment of the investment asset is required, before using borrowed funds. Always consult a professional adviser before you invest using borrowed funds. Using borrowed funds also multiplies gains and losses in the underlying investment. Consider the following options.

Geared Investing

The following example illustrates what happens if you borrow $90,000 for a geared investment with a 10 per cent deposit of your own to invest.

	If you have a 10% Gain	If you have a 10% Loss
Your money (deposit)	10,000	10,000
Borrowed Funds	90,000	90,000
Amount Invested	100,000	100,000
Net value at end of first year	110,000	90,000
Your equity	20,000	Nil
Minus the interest cost (7%)	−6,300	−6,300
Net result	13,700	−16,300 loss

Geared investments can be defined as good debt because you are using borrowed funds to grow your wealth. However, a thorough understanding of the risks associated with this type of investing is important. In the above example you can see how poor investment performance can destroy your equity in an investment. Determining what is a suitable investment requires an assessment of the income stream that is likely to be generated, along with the expected capital growth. When considering a geared investment, always consult a professional adviser who is not associated with the investment. This is especially worth doing in the case of buying real estate in markets you are not familiar with.

Bad Debt

Bad debt can be defined as debt which is not for the purposes of purchasing an appreciating asset. Purchasing on credit any asset which doesn't produce an income stream or grow in value (such as a car or boat) is bad debt. Credit card debt is a bad debt, and so are hire purchase agreements for consumer goods. Buying vacant land could also be classified as a bad debt, unless it is in a prime location. Car debt is bad debt as a car depreciates faster than your loan balance, leaving you with a debt that is greater than the value of the car. Borrowing for a holiday should be avoided, as you must pay for your holiday over a long time.

Interest Free Periods

If you believe department stores are going to allow you to purchase some goods with a six-month interest free period and it will not cost you anything then you are reading the wrong book!

An 'interest free period' means that for the first six months you will not pay interest on the goods you have bought. On the seventh month you receive your bill and the interest charged is often at very high rates, in some cases 20 per cent to 32 per cent. Nothing is free and you are paying high interest rate costs to cover the cost of the goods you held for six months at no charge. Beware! Always read any contract you sign and know exactly what rates of interest you will be expected to pay. Don't allow yourself to fall victim to one of these campaigns, which are designed to generate sales when retail sales are low. If it sounds too good to be true, then it probably is. If you have completed your budget then you won't get caught in these interest rate scams, because you'll only purchase items when you have the funds to do so. Remember – you are in control of your own financial destiny.

Cars

Purchasing cars is an area where many people end up with debt and repayments beyond their comfort level. Most people have to borrow money when they buy a new car. There are steps you can take to ensure you don't end up paying too much for the car you need. First, before you go car shopping, do some research using car magazines and the motoring sections of your local papers to find out which are the critically acclaimed models.

Some people decide on a specific make and model without taking into consideration the running costs. This is particularly worth thinking about if you are considering purchasing a four-wheel drive. In terms of value for money you may see a four-wheel drive as a great option, but the costs of insurance, petrol, servicing, wear and tear on tyres is always going to be much higher than for smaller, more economic vehicles. Ensure the cars you are considering meet your needs and are not just about boosting your ego. Don't trade in your car too frequently as this will create unnecessary stress on your finances. Low-mileage used models can offer you great savings over new models, and all financing options remain open to near-new vehicles. Finally, familiarise yourself with the market place, as car salespeople are experienced at generating commitment from customers.

In terms of financing for private use, borrowing options include personal loans, car loans from banks, car loans from finance companies (hire purchase) and **leasing** arrangements. Jonathan has a strong belief that leasing arrangements are more suitable for buyers who derive a tax benefit from the leasing arrangement. The same applies to hire purchase arrangements, especially those that involve a **balloon payment** at the end of the term. It is hard to see why people who cannot afford to service a personal loan for the whole amount of a car believe that at the end of three years, they'll have saved 30 per cent to 50 per cent of the original cost of the car, and be able to afford to pay the **residual** amount. If you are not in a position to derive a tax benefit, stay away from these financing arrangements. They only encourage you to buy a more expensive car than you would otherwise have selected.

For example, imagine you take out a three-year lease on a $30,000 car at 8 per cent with a 50 per cent residual or final payment. This will cost you $490 per month, with a $15,000 balloon at the end of the term. In order to pay the balloon payment you will need to save an additional $400 per month, assuming a bank interest rate of 4 per cent.

A common sales strategy when car sales drop is for manufacturers to let you pay half now, and pay the balance in a year. It is very tempting if you have managed to save $15,000 or $16,000 to go and get a $30,000 car on one of these deals. These deals are only suitable if you have the whole $30,000 at the start, then you as the buyer can invest the amount of the second payment until it falls due in 12 months.

If you are able to derive a tax benefit by financing a vehicle through a leasing or a commercial hire purchase arrangement, don't pay cash for your car, because it is not economical. That money can be invested, adding valuable income to your household. Part of it can be used to pay the residual amount off the leasing arrangement at the end of the term if you want to keep the car. This is a complex area and you should discuss the alternatives with your tax accountant.

Walter

Walter recently saved $45,000 and bought a car, even though he could have derived a tax benefit from leasing the vehicle. The cost of this missed opportunity was significant, as those funds could have been used to reduce his non tax-deductible home mortgage debt. The benefit could have been further enhanced if the car was leased on an operating lease, including all servicing, tyres, registration, and fuel costs, so that he was effectively paying these costs from pre-tax dollars. In the end Walter paid an additional $9000 per annum by buying the car instead of leasing.

If you are finding your car repayments are too high and you can barely afford to live, then you need to consider the following options:

- sell the car or cancel the lease and buy a cheaper car or use public transport
- renegotiate the loan, increase the term of the loan
- earn more money by obtaining a pay rise, promotion or getting a second job.

Youth Debt

Young people are a major target for financial institutions seeking to increase their consumer lending. Marketers are great at communicating to young people exactly what they want to hear; save 50 per cent off recommended retail price or you can pay it off with regular repayments on 12 months interest free terms. Two areas of particular concern are credit cards and mobile phone contracts.

It is hard to believe that many teenagers are using bankruptcy provisions to extricate themselves from the cycle of credit card debt. Young people are attracted to mobile phone contracts by offers of low monthly access fees and free phones. But what they get in some cases is an 18-month contract with high call costs designed to maximise profits for the phone company. If you need a mobile phone (i.e. you can't make do with a **phone card**) you should look for **prepaid phone contracts** or second hand phones (where you get a **sim card** purchased separately) with no monthly access and no minimum spend with cheap call costs.

If you are a young person going on to further education or starting a first job, our advice is to save as much of your wage as possible and ensure you have plans and goals for the future. Don't be drawn into debt as soon as you leave school by purchasing a new car on hire purchase or allowing yourself to become a credit card junkie and accruing high debt. Adopt healthy shopping patterns by allocating a percentage of your income every week into different categories. These include:

- savings
- clothing
- entertainment
- living expenses (e.g. rent, payment to parents)
- education
- transport
- health – sport, gym membership, etc.
- if you have debt, debt reduction

Make sure the first category is savings and that you save a minimum of 10 per cent of your income. If you are fortunate enough to live at home, your savings should be substantially higher. Once you have saved a substantial amount look for investments that will grow your savings into a nest egg for the future. It is unwise to save large sums of money and then spend them, for example, on buying a new TV set. All of your effort is wasted as this is a dead asset and you will never gain any growth from this purchase.

When you have a small amount of money to invest you should examine diversified **managed funds** as an option. Your local bank or financial institution employees can assist you to decide what is an appropriate investment. Of all the investment classes an investment in your education will yield the best results.

If you can adopt the same strategy discussed in Chapter 3 Budgeting of using a credit card to pay for your living costs, without creating debt, then it is safe to own a credit card. If you are unable to control your spending we would suggest you don't obtain one. The longer you can live without a credit card the better off you will be. Credit cards are a debt trap enabling people to spend money on unnecessary items. If you can save at a young age you will reap the rewards in later years.

Managing Your Mortgage

A home mortgage is probably going to be the largest debt you will acquire. Buying your own home is an emotional purchase. It enables you to feel safe and secure in an environment you create. One of the benefits of a mortgage is it forces you to save a large quantity of your salary and hopefully acquire an asset that will increase in value over the years.

Consider for a moment the costs associated with purchasing and maintaining a home. Costs include the deposit, lawyer fees, stamp duty and rates. The cost of your mortgage should not exceed more than 25–35 per cent of your **gross (pre-tax) household income**. This means if there are two working adults in the household, their combined gross incomes should be added and multiplied by 30 per cent to work out a reasonable mortgage payment.

$$\text{Gross Annual Income (pre-tax)} \times 0.30 =$$
$$\text{Reasonable mortgage repayment}$$

To work out what percentage of your wage you pay to your mortgage you need to divide the repayment by your gross income.

For example:

Sam's wage is $50,000 (gross annual income pre-tax).
His weekly home loan payment is $300.
His yearly home loan payment is $15,600 (300 x 52 =).
To calculate if his current home loan exceeds 35% of his income:
15,600 divided by 50,000 (pre-tax income) = 31.2%
Sam's home loan falls within the reasonable range.

If after this calculation you learn that your mortgage is costing more than 35 per cent of your wage then you need to make a decision about whether or not you can service this high level of debt and still maintain a comfortable life. Some options you may need to consider are:

- Can you sell the property?
- Can you move out to cheaper accommodation and rent out the property?
- Are both spouses working? If not, could other spouse seek employment?
- Can you rent out rooms?
- Can you renegotiate your loan with the bank?
- Look at other outgoings and reassess budget – can you make cutbacks to other areas?
- Can you earn a promotion for more money or get a second job?

Paying Off Your Mortgage Quickly

Once you have completed this exercise, check that your repayments do not exceed more than 30 per cent of your annual income. If they do, you need to devise a strategy that will enable you to pay off your home at a faster rate. Such a strategy is also good for those who wish to pay their mortgage off within a specific time period, but do not know how to organise their finances to achieve this goal. Consider the following:

- Make extra repayments if your home loan allows this flexibility.
- Some financial institutions set specific limits on additional repayments when your mortgage is fixed. In these circumstances, open a **cash management account** and save the money you were planning on paying off your mortgage

into the account until you are permitted to repay the principal.
- Pay other high interest debts off first then focus on your home loan.
- Another option that is only suitable for people who have secure employment, life insurance and income protection insurance is to use the equity in your home to invest into geared investments. These investments can include shares, managed funds, **listed property trusts** and property. The interest costs associated with this investment are tax deductible. The goal is to pay interest only on those borrowed funds using the income generated from the investment as extra repayments for your home loan. As you create more equity in your home, you may borrow more. The risks associated with this strategy are the same as with any other geared investment. Gearing multiplies gains as well as losses. You need to make sure you can pay your interest bill every month. If you decide to use this option ensure you speak with a financial professional before you do anything. It is also important that you have adequate insurance in case you become ill, injured or die.

The impact of extra repayments on a home mortgage is similar to the effect on credit card debt, but because the numbers involved are so much larger then the impact on your life can be substantial:

- If you have two incomes ($50,000 each) coming into the household then you could allocate one wage to be deposited into the home loan account every pay period. In this case the repayment is triple the required minimum repayment. If you calculate the difference in term of the home loan on a $150,000 loan it means you could pay this loan off in less than four years as opposed to 25 years.
- By making fortnightly payments of half your monthly repayment instead of monthly payments you can reduce the term of a standard loan to eight years and save a fortune in interest.
- If interest rates are low use the extra cash to pay off your mortgage faster. Don't spend extra available money on purchasing new goods.

In addition, when interest rates are low, consider fixing half of your outstanding mortgage at either a three or five year interest rate. This will reduce the impact of rising rates across the interest rate cycle. Don't fix all of your mortgage at one rate as most lenders will not allow fixed rate mortgages to be paid off at a faster rate.

For further information on real estate see Chapter 7, Investing.

Summary

- You can achieve the ultimate goal of debt wisdom, leading to financial planning and freedom from debt.
- Never place yourself in a position where your only financial strategy is based on good luck, such as winning the lottery.
- High levels of debt can create problems within relationships.
- Don't live beyond your means by spending money you don't have.
- Create your own financial destiny.
- Understand the difference between a need and a want.
- Living with positive Money Karma means you know what will make you happy.
- You should know how close to bankruptcy you may be.
- The key to success is to have clearly defined goals and self-discipline.
- Allocate more than the minimum repayment to clear credit card debt.
- Pay off high interest rate credit card debt first.
- Take one day at a time when paying off debt, setting yourself realistic goals.
- Ensure you meet your financial responsibilities with integrity.
- Always consult a Certified Financial Planner (CFP) before implementing any major financial decisions.
- Purchasing an asset which doesn't produce any income stream or grow in value is a non-productive investment.
- Leasing arrangements are suitable for buyers who derive a tax benefit from the leasing arrangement.
- Mortgage repayments should never exceed more than 25–35 per cent of your gross (pre-tax) household income.
- Don't use equity in your home to purchase goods from which you cannot derive an income.

5

Gambling

He was a self-made man who owed his lack of success to nobody

— Joseph Heller (1923–2001)

When introducing positive Money Karma into your life, it is important to examine what constitutes gambling and the effects gambling may have on your budget and overall happiness. We define gambling as any activity in which you spend money in the hope of generating money or prizes, but where the outcome is unknown. It includes day trading on the stock exchange, going to a casino, using poker or slot machines or purchasing lottery and scratch and win tickets. For many of us, gambling may not be an issue, but there are a growing number of individuals who are unable to break their destructive habit. The Gamblers Anonymous Association of America describe problem gambling as an illness that leads to financial and personal problems. Gambling is a behaviour which will always be part of a gambler's profile, but you can learn techniques that will stop you from gambling. To learn more you can join Gamblers Anonymous.

The life of a problem gambler is not pleasant. You live your life in a cycle of deceit. You deceive your family, friends and most of all yourself. You spend money you don't have, you often lose it and then try to make up for it by betting more money in an effort to recoup it. The physical and emotional pressure you place yourself under often causes severe depression and, for some, suicidal thoughts. If gambling is an issue for you, you can empower yourself by seeking help. Listed below is a set of questions designed by Gamblers Anonymous, which may help you to determine whether or not you are in the compulsive gambler category.

> *A moment of time may make us unhappy forever.*
> — JOHN GAY (1685–1732)

> *When sorrows come, they come not single spies, but in battalions.*
> — HAMLET, WILLIAM SHAKESPEARE (1564–1616)

Could You be a Problem Gambler?

1. Did you ever lose time from work or study due to gambling?
2. Has gambling ever made your home life unhappy?
3. Did gambling affect your reputation?
4. Did you ever gamble to get money with which to pay debts or otherwise solve financial difficulties?
5. Did gambling cause a decrease in your ambition or efficiency?
6. Have you ever felt remorse after gambling?
7. After losing did you feel you must return as soon as possible and win back your losses?
8. After a win did you have a strong urge to return and win more?
9. Did you ever gamble until your last dollar was gone?
10. Did you ever borrow to finance your gambling?
11. Have you ever sold anything to finance gambling?
12. Were you reluctant to use gambling money for normal expenditures?
13. Did gambling make you careless of the welfare of yourself or your family?
14. Did you ever gamble longer than you had planned?
15. Have you ever gambled to escape worry or trouble?
16. Have you ever committed, or considered committing, an illegal act to finance gambling?
17. Did gambling cause you to have difficulty in sleeping?
18. Do arguments, disappointments or frustrations create within you an urge to gamble?
19. Did you ever have an urge to celebrate any good fortune by a few hours of gambling?
20. Have you ever considered self-destruction or suicide as a result of your gambling?

Most compulsive gamblers will answer yes to at least seven of these questions – we urge you to seek help now if you have done so. This is your opportunity to empower yourself and stop the cycle of debt affecting your life.

Lottery Tickets, Poker and Slot Machines

There are people in the community who would not be classified as problem gamblers, but who spend large amounts of money gambling, in an effort to win prizes such as cars, boats or cash. The most common methods of gambling these people use are lotteries, poker and slot machines. The majority of funds put into poker and slot machines are returned to the gambling venue or paid in taxes back to the government. These taxes are then used by the government to build new roads, schools and other infrastructure. That is why governments have generally been increasing the number of gambling licences and allowing a proliferation of new gaming venues. The odds of winning a major lottery are minute (about the same as being struck by lightning) – you would profit more by saving the cost of the tickets and investing it. There is nothing wrong with buying the weekly lottery ticket, but be aware of what you are spending. If you then put your spare change through the poker machines, you may be spending a considerable amount of money.

You may think the odd lottery ticket does not cost you much, but have you ever consciously thought of what you are spending?

- How many scratch-and-win tickets do you buy a week?
- What is the average cost?
- How many lotteries/raffles do you enter?
- How much money do you put through a poker or slot machine weekly?
- Some machines take anywhere from a few cents up to large amounts of cash.
- Do you have a set amount within your budget used only for slot or poker machines?
- Throughout your life what has been your total winnings from gambling?

At the end of this chapter is a Gambling Expenditure Chart which you can complete to assess the pattern of your current spending on gambling. You also need to consider the amount of money you spend on drinks, food including snack foods and the cost of transport to get to and from venues. Include this amount in the chart.

- Statistics show poker/slot machines are making the majority of money in suburbs where families are struggling to keep their budgets under control. Venues may have signs advertising morning tea at $2 for senior citizens or $5 lunches, designed to lure the lonely or bored to encourage them to gamble. Be aware that sometimes these economical meals are offered so you feel better about spending money on the poker and slot machines. Don't allow yourself to fall into this trap. If you have a mortgage, a car loan, or credit cards not paid off, and other bills, is it financially responsible to spend your spare change? Remember you are in control of your financial destiny. Take control: don't cut back in all other areas of your budget and waste the savings on gambling.

Buying Raffle Tickets from Charities

There are quite a few charitable organisations that sell raffle tickets offering large prizes such as million-dollar homes fully furnished, money, cars or holidays. While there is nothing wrong with purchasing these tickets, always consider the amount of money you are spending on a monthly basis. Most charities offer automatic credit card deductions for each new raffle. They ask you for your permission, at the same time telling you that you don't want to miss out on winning the prize. Are you aware of how many tickets you are buying each month? Have you included this in your budget? Do you even know anything about the charity you are investing in? If you do not know what you are spending then you need to assess how much money you spend yearly.

Part of the Money Karma philosophy includes making a viable contribution to society. Chapter 6 will show you how to make a donation to the charity of your choice on a regular basis without ruining your budget.

Day Trading

An emerging type of investor over the last four or five years is the day trader. This is somebody who buys and sells stocks daily in order to make regular small profits. Typically day traders trade on the Internet, usually without the traditional research and support that stockbrokers have at their disposal. Often these traders have little understanding or knowledge of the companies they buy and sell. The main requirement for a stock to be of interest to a day trader is a high degree of volatility. Day trading is fundamentally dangerous because it requires the trader to make significantly more profitable decisions than unprofitable decisions. Often the trader has to cover the transaction cost, as well as making a profit on the day. Such costs could be substantial, especially when making multiple transactions.

Many day traders obtain their stock information from chat rooms on the Internet or from friends and relatives who may have heard of a hot tip. In effect this is a form of gambling, as you have no idea of the fundamental quality of the investments; nor do you have any expectation of holding the stock for a reasonable period of time. This makes the activity inherently speculative. We classify this practice as gambling. To read more about understanding the stock market refer to Chapter 7, Investing.

Other forms of gambling include:

- horse racing
- going to the trots
- betting on dogs
- poker games/cards
- going to casinos
- betting on football, soccer, cricket and even the Olympics.
- calling TV stations to enter competitions or become a contestant charged per call.
- Internet gambling or Internet competitions where a fee to register is involved.
- bingo/Keno.

This list is endless. Behaviour which causes you to spend or speculate with money, winning prizes or cash is detrimental to establishing a financially secure future. The money you choose to waste on gambling is money you could be using to secure a comfortable retirement. You don't know when you may lose your job. Losing your hard-earned cash with the faint hope of winning a large prize does not make financial sense.

As an example of how much money you are spending each week, consider the calculation below:

$20 per week for 20 years in a managed fund returning 8% = $51,050
$20 per week for 20 years in a bank account returning 4% = $25,500

If you have a partner who has a gambling problem you need to help them seek assistance so they can eventually help themselves. Don't allow them access to your savings or any other accounts. Be in control and don't allow this illness to destroy your livelihood or family. Always remember you are not alone and there are many associations that can assist gamblers and their families with counselling.

Everyone spends differently. If you want to gamble and you can control the amount you spend on it, you can build it into your budget. But if you can't control yourself and you have debts or are placing your financial future in risk, you need to acknowledge this and change. The only factor holding you back from living with positive Money Karma is yourself.

Gambling Expenditure Chart

Type of gambling:	fill in the various ways you choose to gamble.
Weekly cost:	what you spend on gambling every week.
Monthly cost:	if you only gamble once a month, the cost monthly.
Food and drinks:	the money spent on food and drinks while gambling.
Transport:	the cost of transport to and from the gambling venue whether you go by bus, train, plane, taxi or private motor vehicle.
Winnings:	how much you have **won** each week or month
Savings:	how much you have **saved** from each weekly or monthly gambling win. Do you save any or just gamble the winnings?
Total cost:	actual spending for the week or month gambling. If you won any money it comes off the total cost for that week.

Type of Gambling	Weekly Cost	Monthly Cost	Food Drinks	Transport	Winnings	Saved From Winnings and Invested	Total Cost
Lottery Ticket (example)	$7				nil		−$7
Slot/Poker Machine (example)	$50		$25	$15 (taxi)	$5	nil	−$90
						Total:	$97

Keep this chart for a full year by adding more rows.

Summary

- It is important to examine what constitutes gambling and the effects gambling may have on your budget, family and overall happiness.
- Gambling is any activity in which you spend money in the hope of generating money or prizes, but where the outcome is unknown.
- Gamblers Anonymous describe problem gambling as an illness that leads to personal and financial problems.
- You are in control of your financial destiny: don't cut back in all other areas of your budget and waste the savings on gambling.

6

Relationships

If a man's character is to be abused, say what you will, there's nobody like a relation to do the business.

— *Vanity Fair*, William Thackeray (1811–63)

> There is scarcely any less trouble in running a family than there is in governing an entire state... and domestic matters are no less importunate for being less important.
>
> — MICHEL DE MONTAIGNE (1533–92)

A discussion on how to manage one's finances would be incomplete without an understanding of the effects different relationships have on your financial wellbeing. Sharing your life with those you love can at times fill your life with immense joy and at other times cause you incredible grief. Often problems start with financial issues, as each partner has different expectations and experiences with the way they manage their finances.

Money means different things to different people. Some of us get our pay cheques and put it into retirement funds, the stock market and growth areas, while still having some left over for our daily living expenses. Others receive their pay cheque and use this money for expensive meals out, an opportunity to buy a new outfit and enjoy themselves until the next cheque. They are electing to live for the moment and do not feel the need to worry about the future.

The way you choose to respect your money today will have an effect on how you live tomorrow. As with relationships, managing money requires a balanced approach. To have success with money and your relationship, you need to design a plan that will assist you to reach your financial, personal, career and lifestyle goals. Your plan could be based on the Money Karma Quadrant (page 18). You must attend to all areas to ensure your life is happy and well balanced.

The positive principle underlying this challenge is that we should try to behave in a loving, friendly and compassionate manner. We should create an atmosphere of honesty and openness so that whenever the issue of money and financial management is raised, neither partner is subjected to negative emotions. You must learn to value each other's opinions and always make your decisions together. Often the cause of unhappiness is one partner blaming the other for the poor state of any joint financial affairs. Remember, we are all brought up differently, come from different backgrounds (and sometimes different cultures) and have different expectations.

It is always important to work together as a team when designing your financial plan so that it incorporates both partners' wishes for the future. This theory also applies to families, who often neglect to include their children in financial goal setting. Including your children in this process educates them about the value of money and the importance of work and saving.

With one in two marriages breaking down, it is fair to predict that many children will grow up in single parent homes. If you want your children to have the best opportunities, both parents need to contribute financially and emotionally.

Couples

To maintain a successful relationship, including in financial matters, it is imperative that both partners understand the goals each person wishes to achieve. This means that you are both actively involved when designing and planning a budget. A relationship will not succeed if one member is in control when it comes to deciding how money is to be saved and spent. All bankbooks, cheque books, retirement fund balances, wills, stocks held, insurance papers and mortgages etc. should be kept in a safe place which both parties can access. If you have no idea where your financial documents are, or what amounts of money are held in accounts, then you need to find out and take responsibility for this aspect of your life. If your files are kept electronically (on the computer), it is important that both partners have passwords and access to this information.

The second stage in this process requires you both to set aside a specific time every month or week to discuss goals and planning. As you are embarking on a new course in your life to create balance within your financial situation, now is the time for you both to take the opportunity to be totally honest about your spending patterns. If either of you has a debt that you have been concealing from the other, due to fear of reprisal, get it out in the open now. Remember, you are both expected to be totally honest and compassionate with each other.

You both need to recognise the problem by working out a solution by which you can get rid of the debt. Arguments relating to money cause bad Money Karma, and in turn your partner may not be totally honest with you. If you choose to argue over how you spend your money, you will be unable to balance the financial side of your relationship, due to negative emotions raised when this issue is discussed.

Now you should write down your goals, each with a deadline. To achieve your goals you'll need to make some sacrifices. This is your opportunity to discuss where cut backs will be made. Include the following topics in your planning process:

- retirement planning
- educational planning
- mortgage elimination
- savings
- holidays
- charitable donations
- wills and estate planning

Both of you must take control of different areas within your budget. It is unfair to place the burden of all financial management with one partner. Suggesting the excuse that you don't have the time is not valid. Neither is saying 'I am no good with finances'. Purchase a calculator to assist you with calculations.

Empowering yourself with positive Money Karma demonstrates you understand what you are working towards, and how long each financial commitment you have made will take to pay off. Refer to Chapter 2, The Subconscious Mind for goal-setting strategies and to Chapter 3, Budgeting.

Having Children?

A difficult decision couples have to agree on is whether or not they are going to have children, and if so, how many. Society has become more accepting of the realisation that couples who marry or live together no longer commit to each other just to have children. It has been estimated that approximately 25 per cent of women living in Western society will not have children. This has been attributed to increasing levels of education and career prospects available to women today. Another factor influencing this decision is the commitment and cost associated with educating and caring for children.

It is estimated that the average cost of raising a child is approximately $150,000 to $250,000. If you intend educating your child in a private school then the cost increases by anywhere from $100,000 to $350,000, depending on the age they start attending and the cost for your choice of education. The Australian Institute of Family Studies states that as a child ages, it costs more. Their studies have also shown that higher income families tend to spend more on their children.

When planning to have children, if a parent intends to stay home once the baby is born, income levels decrease. A family budget reduced from two wages to one can become very difficult to manage if you have not planned your financial strategy.

If you are paying off a mortgage, car and other debts, will you have the necessary funds available to maintain a comfortable family budget after the baby is born? We recommend that before you consider starting a family, you ensure that your mortgage is manageable. We suggest that you also clear all of your credit card debt, and reduce your motor vehicle costs, if you are still paying off a car loan. Having a child is a special moment for any family. To really enjoy your new baby, don't start the journey to parenthood with negative Money Karma.

Also consider your current standard of living before you have children. To maintain this standard a couple with three dependent children will require between 33 per cent and 73 per cent more income than a childless couple.

In reality there is no single figure which clearly defines the actual cost of raising children, because there are varying standards of living. Only you can estimate an accurate financial figure of what it will cost to raise your child. It is important both parents agree on a financial plan for your child's welfare without sacrificing a comfortable lifestyle and creating an unmanageable budget.

Planning for Children

When planning for a family it is a good idea to learn to live on one wage. Use the other wage to pay off the mortgage and other debts. This will ensure you have reduced these debts substantially before you begin parenting. Begin working out a financial strategy to assist you with meeting all of your goals. This includes working out a checklist:

- What will your mortgage be reduced to before the baby is born?
- What is your current mortgage balance, credit card debt and car payments?
- Have you selected and budgeted for the best health insurance for the pregnant woman? (Note that to be eligible to claim costs associated with the pregnancy, you need to be Insured for a period before conception.)
- Do you have disability insurance for mother in case of complications during or after birth?
- Do you have income protection for working spouse and insurance for non-working spouse in case the working spouse has an accident?
- For what length of time do you plan to live on one wage?
- What are you prepared to eliminate from your current lifestyle to accommodate costs associated with the new baby?
- What costs are associated with childcare if both parents are working?
- What amount needs to be spent on new furniture etc. for the baby?
- Have both parents prepared a will and have you planned how to handle your estate to protect your child's future welfare?
- How much will you need to save for your child's education? (Will it be private/ public, and if private, at what age will they begin?)

Note: Always read the fine print of any documents before you obtain any insurance or sign any contracts.

Families

Many parents fail to include their children in the planning of a family budget. Later, they wonder why their offspring practise poor money habits. It is the responsibility of parents to teach their children the fundamentals of working, saving and developing an understanding of financial management. If you start educating your children at an early age, you will reduce the level of conflict money matters can cause with teenagers later in life.

Set aside a specific night every week or month and declare it will be the family budget night. This time must never be broken as you are trying to reinforce the 'value of money' ethic. Create an environment of openness by allowing everyone to speak and ask questions. This experience should be enjoyable and looked forward to. Every member of the family should be present and, from a reasonable age, must be allowed input into the family budget. Family members list their goals, whether they be personal or financial.

Use the Goal Setting Chart from Chapter 2 (page 28) to record the discussion. Each goal must have a deadline. They can then be incorporated into the Family Budget List of Goals. Your children should understand that the income you earn is there to pay for living costs. This should reinforce to them the value of money. It helps if children understand how the family budget works. Plan for family holidays on this chart and regularly save over the year for these events. When you have a specific target children understand why you can't waste money on buying unplanned purchases. We suggest children be given their allowance at these sessions.

Checklist for Successful Family Budgeting

- Use the Money Karma Quadrant (page 18) to prioritise goals.
- Fill out the Family Budget List of Goals and have it on display.
- Include children in the family budget planning process.
- Place a job list with children's names and jobs to be completed somewhere that children can easily check it.
- Children must have an allowance they earn, and it should be increased according to age.

- Always have a grocery list before going shopping. This can help decrease impulse buying, it helps reduce wastage and you can estimate the cost of grocery bills.

Remember, set aside a specific night every week or month for budget night and keep it regular.

Family Budget List of Goals

Family Motto
Insert your family's mission statement, for example:
Respect, love and care for each other. Assist those less fortunate, conserve the earth's resources and always act with humanity and compassion

Financial and Personal Goals
Insert goals for each member of family both financial and personal with a deadline, for example:
Mary: save for roller blades (financial)
Peter: learn to play soccer (personal)

Family Holiday this year is: Fill in destination and amount to save (e.g. $10,000).

Refer to the Goal Setting Chart in Chapter 2 (page 28). Insert goals here for your family chart.

Children's Family Job List

Allowance for:

List children's names and amount of allowance, for example:
- *Mary, age 7, weekly allowance is $2*
- *Peter, age 9, weekly allowance is $4*

TASKS	SUN	MON	TUES	WED	THURS	FRI	SAT	COMPLETED
Homework								
Night reading								
Music Practice								
Pick up Toys								
Feed pet								
Fill dog water bowl								
Empty dishwasher								
Clean bedroom								
Empty bins								
Walk dog								
Vacuum bedroom								
Clean bathroom								
Maintain bicycle								
Water garden								
Do something for community								
Bonus*								

Step-families

Blended families are more commonplace in our society today. As with any family unit, there are many financial issues to consider. We suggest that, before you decide to marry or move in with a new partner who has children from a previous relationship, you understand what financial commitments your partner has made for these children, and how your finances together will be arranged. This includes:

- Will you have separate bank accounts or combine incomes, sharing household expenses once living together?
- How will estate planning issues and wills be designed? (If one partner dies will the other be able to live in the house or sell it? Will the estate have to be divided up for other beneficiaries while other partner is still alive)?
- If you marry or live together where will you live? If you own your home what happens with the funds if property is sold or rented?
- How are you prepared to assist with the financial aspects of child support and other financial commitments of your partner?
- How much are child support payments monthly?
- Have children been promised a car or gifts if they graduate from high school or after other education? (The reason you ask is so that you understand what promises have been made with the children before you came into your partner's life).
- Is the former partner receiving any other payments other than child support from your new partner or additional financial support? How much and for how long is it expected to continue?
- Will support payments cease once children are 18 years old or will they continue until they graduate from college, university or other study?

It is important to remember that when you enter into a relationship with children from a previous relationship you are involving yourself with both your new partner and these children. It is advisable to discuss all financial issues at the beginning of this union.

Child-Support Payments

You should always explore your options before you commit to a specific child-support financial strategy. Consider the following:

- Deciding who has custody of a child or children is going to be an emotional decision, but there is a financial aspect to it also. If you have no custody you will pay a subsidy of all the child's living costs and still have to fund a household for yourself.
- Maintenance trusts (which are essentially a trust arrangement where the income and capital from the trust can be distributed for the benefit of your children in a tax effective manner). This option is suitable for people with considerable assets.

If possible, work closely with your former partner to reach a mutually acceptable financial agreement and then involve your lawyers to ensure that it is legally enforceable.

If you are reaching a financial agreement with your partner where the courts are not involved, you should involve a financial planner in this process. Whatever the financial outcome, always remember that your child's welfare must come first. Always act with integrity, honesty, responsibility and love.

> *Experience is the name everyone gives to their mistakes.*
> – OSCAR WILDE
> (1854–1900)

Patrick

Patrick, a father of three, came from a family worth millions of dollars. He worked occasionally, but lived comfortably on an income from his family trust. When Patrick's wife left him, he was able to hire the best divorce lawyers his family could afford. Patrick decided that if his wife was leaving and taking the children, she would have to learn to do it on her own with as little child support as he could legally pay. His lawyers negotiated a deal that meant his taxable income was based on the minimum wage (this includes not being responsible for any medical or dental plans). Patrick ensured that his financial responsibilities ended on his children's 18th birthday regardless of whether they had finished high school or were still in their final year.

Always honour your responsibilities, don't promise your children education or other financial incentives if you have no intention of carrying them out, and don't use the tax system or other legal loopholes to forfeit your financial responsibilities. When you honour your financial responsibilities you create positive Money Karma. It is always advisable to assess all of the responsibilities that are required if you choose to become a parent. If you value money more than your relationships, parenthood may not be the best option for you to take.

Charity

> *In Charity there is no excess.*
> – SIR FRANCIS BACON (1561–1626)

Our perspective of the world is changing in the new millennium, creating an atmosphere of global consciousness. It is essential we develop a deeper understanding of and respect for all life on our planet. We believe that to be truly considerate human beings we must be kind and compassionate, not only for our own wellbeing or our family's, but to friends, community and those whom we do not know. As a compassionate human being, you never actively engage in thoughts or behaviour which cause spiritual or mental anxiety to others, and you remain concerned about the welfare of all living things that inhabit and share our planet. You share these feelings of kindness by actively giving back to our planet, on whose resources we live. Giving back to society means more than just giving a donation to a charitable organisation, but also giving something of yourself to make the world more compassionate and caring. Every kindly deed and thought makes a difference.

We must learn to reconcile our differences as human beings on this earth and start showing each other a more caring and compassionate side, to be accepting of different cultures, belief systems and religions. Some cultures experience the trauma of war, terrorism and fear on a daily basis. These people lose family members, friends and neighbours and they feel and grieve just like anyone else on this planet. We shouldn't need the

> *Compassion is not a sloppy, sentimental feeling for people who are underprivileged or sick … it is an absolutely practical belief that, regardless of a person's background, ability or ability to pay, he should be provided with the best that society has to offer.*
> – NEIL KINNOCK (MAIDEN SPEECH, HOUSE OF COMMONS, 1970)

senseless waste of human life to make us all start listening and acting in a compassionate and caring manner.

We need to begin giving luck to those who may need our assistance. If you have been fortunate enough to have an education, then your duty is to improve opportunities for others who have not had the same benefits. For example, you could make a regular donation to your former school or university to help with their scholarship program or improve facilities, or you could donate to a local library. Once others are helped along the way and become educated, they will be able to pass it on. Charitable acts come in many forms. You may assist someone in the workplace with a difficult task or help an elderly neighbour mow their lawn. You may even just smile or say hello to a stranger. Charity is about being generous with time, spirit, knowledge and compassion, and less focused on judging others and only caring for ourselves. We need to cease being introspective and begin connecting with others, understanding what matters in our lives and what does not.

Ensuring that we create, encourage and live in a society that is compassionate and caring, we should endeavour to make periodical financial contributions to organisations that assist others in need. A society's compassion can be assessed by the care given to those who are less fortunate than ourselves.

Creating positive Money Karma enables you to assist those in need to live more comfortably at the same time as helping them gain skills towards becoming independent. We often think only of ourselves and our needs. People respond positively and are attracted to friendly, kind and caring actions. You gain positive feelings if you act from the heart. Actions speak louder than words. Kindness is returned when you least expect it and often from those you may not have even assisted. There is an old Native American saying: 'Don't judge me until you have walked in my moccasins and experienced life as I have.'

> *If culture means anything, it means knowing what value to set upon human life; it's not somebody with a mortarboard reading Greek. I know a lot of facts, history. That's not culture. Culture is openness of the individual psyche... to the news of being.*
>
> – SAUL BELLOW (*THE GLASGOW HERALD*, 1985)

Health

The successful planning of our finances is impacted by the state of our health, which includes emotional, physical and social wellbeing. Maintaining a healthy body and mind often lowers the probability that later in life there will be financial hardship caused by escalating medical costs. If we neglect our health by regularly indulging in fast foods and avoiding exercise it will be to the detriment of our physical, emotional and financial wellbeing. Heart disease and strokes are the leading cause of death in the developed world. There is increased risk of these diseases in older people, so as our population ages the cost of medical insurance and health care will dramatically increase. If the current rate of heart disease, diet-induced diabetes, obesity and other lifestyle-affected illnesses continue to increase, many of us will be unable to adequately budget for medical costs.

> *It is not to live but to be healthy that makes a life*
> – MARTIAL

As with credit card debt problems, we are given warnings when we are allowing our health to suffer by over-indulging. These warnings start as small signals, such as feeling out of breath as you ascend a staircase, or perhaps carrying extra body weight. If you receive these signals, don't excuse this weight as a part of ageing, it is not. It is a signal that you must begin to care for your health. Regularly program some form of exercise daily, and don't spend leisure time merely watching TV or in other forms of inactive leisure. Regularly reassess your lifestyle pattern. When you maintain a well balanced, healthy lifestyle with regular exercise you eliminate feelings of depression, creating assurance, self-esteem and confidence.

With people working longer hours in an effort to maintain their budget, many of us are no longer cooking healthy meals on a regular basis. Research shows many of us now purchase fast food on the way home from work. These meals are made with high levels of saturated fats, sugar and salt and are adding to the problem of obesity in society today. The solution is to re-examine how you are living and the cost associated with consuming these unhealthy meals regularly. Not only are you placing more pressure on your food budget, but you are guaranteeing an unhealthy old age with high medical costs. Learn to eat healthily. There are many nutritional recipe books published which you could buy to educate yourself.

> *Look at your health; and if you have it, praise God, and value it next to a good conscience; for health is the second blessing that we mortals are capable of; a blessing money cannot buy.*
> — IZAAK WALTON (1593–1683)

There are other areas we ignore when speaking of physical wellbeing and this includes dental care. For every sugary drink, fruit juice, candy bar, sweet, biscuit or cookie you consume your teeth are being subjected to possible decay.

Health is a major component of the Money Karma Quadrant as a healthy body assists us to reduce stress levels. What you eat affects your emotional and physical wellbeing and with an understanding of regular, healthy eating an individual's self-esteem increases, which further enhances relationships.

Prevention rather than cure is the key to developing a healthy body and mind. Listed below is a table with a guide to suggested height and weight measurements. This chart is based on Body Mass Index (BMI). Always consult a doctor before undertaking a major change in how you exercise or a new diet.

Suggested Height For Weight Chart

For men and women aged 18 and over. Based on Body Mass Index (BMI).

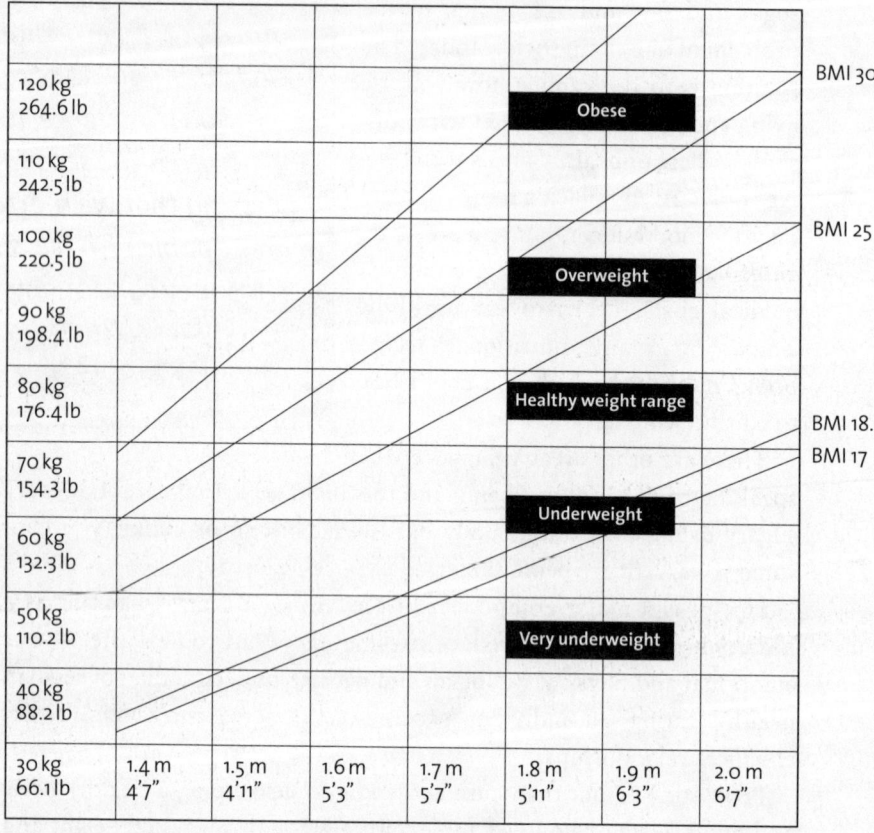

(Height) Metres/Feet

Source: Australian Nutrition Foundation

Self-discipline is the key to maintaining a healthy body and securing a financial future free from unplanned medical costs. Lack of exercise increases the level of negative energy within our bodies, giving us no outlet to rid ourselves of stressful emotions. Living with nature and having a body that is healthy allows us to live with balance in all quadrants of our life.

Summary

- Couples must learn to value each other's opinion and always make decisions together.
- Always include your children in family financial goal setting discussions. It is the parent's responsibility to teach children about the importance of work, saving and money.
- Set a specific time aside every month or week to discuss family goals and financial planning.
- All family goals must be written down with a deadline.
- Don't place the burden of all financial management on one partner.
- It is never an excuse to say you must relinquish your financial responsibilities because you are no good with finances.
- When entering into a relationship with a partner who has children from a previous relationship, ensure you understand what financial commitments your partner has made for these children.
- Always honour your financial responsibilities and remember child support payments are necessary for the welfare of your child.
- A society's compassion can be measured by the care given to those who are less fortunate than ourselves.
- Self-discipline is the key to maintaining a healthy body and securing a financial future free from unplanned medical costs.

> *Better to hunt in fields, for health unbought, than fee the doctor for a nauseous draught. The wise cure, on exercise depend; God never made his work for man to mend.*
>
> — JOHN DRYDEN
> (1631–1700)

⑦ Investing

*Man **must** choose whether to be rich in things or in the freedom to use them.*
— Deschooling Society, Ivan Illich (1971)

> *[On being told his request for a loan had been granted]*
> *I don't trust a bank that would lend money to such a poor risk.*
>
> — ROBERT BENCHLEY
> (1889–1945)

When designing your financial plan it is crucial that you seek appropriate investment advice. Don't make major decisions without completely understanding the type of investments you have selected. Investing wisely requires you to be a proactive participant and not reactive when your investment may be affected by adverse financial conditions. Ensure you understand what fluctuations in the marketplace may affect your investment by placing your investments with money market experts (who are professionals in this field). You can substantially limit your risk and stress levels.

How to Select a Professional Financial Adviser

A difficult financial decision people have to make is who to take financial advice from and who to entrust with your personal wealth. Selecting a financial adviser is like choosing a doctor or lawyer. First, always ask your friends or family for a recommendation. When selecting an adviser you should feel at ease and able to communicate freely without any apprehension. Whenever you don't understand something, always ask for clarification. A good adviser should ensure you understand all investment recommendations. Should you feel intimidated or unable to communicate freely with the adviser then this is not the right person for you to invest with. It is essential that your adviser design an investment strategy that meets all your requirements. We recommend you always see at least two advisers when deciding to whom to entrust your money. Remember it is your money and you have total control over what happens to it. Listed below is a checklist that you should find helpful when selecting your financial adviser.

Financial Adviser Checklist

(Tick each criterion matched when selecting a financial adviser. You should have at least seven ticks to ensure you have selected a professional financial adviser.)

Mandatory Requirement	Yes	No
Qualified Certified Financial Planner (CFP)		
University/College Degree		
Engages your trust		
Plan tailored for your needs		
Strategic life plan		
Clear fee disclosure in dollar terms, not just as a percentage		
You understand total cost of entry and exit fees for each investment strategy		
Full disclosure of commission and if adviser has any restrictions on which products can be sold		
Only use a discretionary service if client does not have capacity for themselves		

It is imperative to select a financial adviser who can demonstrate a depth of thinking with strategy options. Always make yourself familiar with the recommendations. Beware of advisers who only want to sell a particular product. Some advisers receive weighted commissions to encourage them to recommend specific investments over others. This practice is known to be prevalent in some financial institutions where various products carry more commission than others, encouraging the recommendation of the inhouse products.

Often clients choose the cheapest financial adviser in the belief they will save themselves money. Don't fall for this false economy, as all financial advisers are different. You don't choose a lawyer, doctor or accountant just because their fees are less. Select these professionals on the basis of the quality of advice. Selecting a financial adviser is no different as you are paying for a strategic financial plan, ensuring you have the funds necessary to meet your specific goal. The old adage, you get what you pay for, is apt.

Warning Signs

When you have received your plan, and you want to proceed to invest your funds (as per agreement), ensure when your financial adviser requests you to sign a cheque your name is there. Do not write the cheque out with your adviser's name on it even though he/she may say he will transfer it into your name later. When you are signing your cheque it should be in the name of the fund manager and your name should be next to it. For example, if the fund manager's name is Secure Funds Investments, the cheque should read 'Secure Funds Investments — (Insert your name here)'. If you just write the name 'Secure Funds Investments' then if your financial adviser is unethical he/she could simply fill in their name after 'Secure Funds Investments'.

Other warning signs include:

- You feel as though you are being pressured to sign over your money to the adviser.
- There is only a limited time to invest, for example, you may be told if you don't sign up today, you'll miss out on earning a substantial return on your investment.
- You are given rates of return that are ridiculously high or too good to be true (then they are).

If you select a financial adviser and the investment strategies offered to you are limited to real estate strategies or tax minimisation strategies, you should seek another adviser. People who do this are product sales people and not financial professionals. An experienced professional should be able to provide advice about investments in all asset classes. A prudent risk management strategy demands that investments be made across a number of asset classes. If you're having trouble finding a good financial planner, try your local Financial Planners/Services Association website, which will direct you to your nearest registered financial adviser.

When deciding what financial advice to take, it is always advisable to consider the adviser's education and the quality of advice being given. If you elect to take advice from a person who has no formal training or experience within the financial sector, and who has never earned a living by providing financial advice, you are the only person to blame if your financial affairs cause you problems later. Some of us choose to take tips or financial suggestions from family and friends who have little understanding of the consequences that poor financial advice can have.

It is important to know the length of time this adviser has been giving financial advice so that you are not left in a position where your financial future is planned by someone with limited experience. In addition, consider the professionalism of an organisation which allows an inexperienced financial planner to work with clients who are paying fees whether the adviser is experienced or not.

Understand that some inexperienced financial advisers who may have worked in banks, insurance or credit unions often claim to have been in the financial services industry. The term 'financial services industry' can mean working as a bank teller, mobile home lender or in customer services. This is not adequate experience for a qualified financial planner.

Some common acronyms used by financial planners include:

CFP: Certified Financial Planner (This is the highest qualification)
DFP: Diploma of Financial Planning
ASIA: Associate Securities Institute of Australia, signifies completion of a Graduate Diploma
Grad Dip Fin Plan: Graduate Diploma of Financial Planning
CPA: Certified Practising Accountant
B Economics: Bachelor of Economics
B Commerce: Business Degree
BA: Bachelor of Arts

These are just a few of the qualifications held by Certified Financial Planners. Many hold degrees from a variety of different disciplines.

Finally, only a qualified, experienced financial professional can determine what are the right options for you, and the security of your money.

The majority of financial advisers are ethical, honest and skilled professionals. You need to ensure that the professional you choose suits you. An experienced, well educated and licensed financial adviser should assist you to:

- make well informed decisions about your wealth
- use your money, debt, assets etc. to your best advantage
- select investments which will meet your specific needs and goals.

Source: Financial Planning Association

Selecting Investments

When selecting an investment portfolio, it is important to hold a variety of different asset classes so you can manage portfolio risk, thus ensuring liquidity (being able to access funds readily) is not a concern. Some of us select investments that are inappropriate for our circumstances or time frames.

Many investors choose to invest in one asset class consisting of either property or shares, and while the asset class performs, the investor is usually satisfied. However, when the investments cease performing, the danger of investing in one asset class becomes apparent, as there may be declining investment income, non-existent growth and extreme volatility, all major issues for the investor. Property investors can face some particularly problematic issues, such as vacancy of rental property (resulting in no rental income) and lack of liquidity. If your current investment strategy involves only one asset class, such as property or shares, you could find yourself in financial difficulty in some circumstances. When investing, it is imperative you design a plan that accommodates your lifestyle and budget.

Different investment asset classes have different characteristics and are categorised as either **income investments** or **growth investments**. Income investments are assets that deliver a known or predictable level of regular income, such as a bank bill, cash deposit, or a government bond. Income investments typically do not enjoy any significant change in capital value over their life, although bonds do have a fluctuating value. Growth investments are those asset classes that enjoy increasing capital value, such as domestic and international shares, and property. You need to construct a portfolio comprising the appropriate mix between the various investment assets. We emphasise the importance of seeking professional financial advice before selecting any investment strategy.

A key concept in investment is diversification. This is the process of purchasing a range of investments within asset classes (e.g. shares, property, fixed interest, cash). The purpose for diversification is to reduce risk within an investment portfolio. It achieves this when the various asset classes have different performance levels and react differently to various economic conditions. The ultimate goal is to construct a balanced portfolio that has a lower risk and a higher performance than can be achieved with a single investment.

Diversification also protects investors from the total failure of an individual investment. Some people may lose their entire life savings in a single investment scheme. If you adhere to the concept of diversification, this is less likely to occur. Although it is impossible to completely protect investors from corporate failures, adherence to diversification and quality will protect investors in most circumstances.

The investment choices you make will have an impact on your lifestyle. If you select an investment strategy that leaves you with a limited budget, with no excess funds for holidays, entertainment and clothing, this will place unnecessary pressure on all relationships, and most of all on your spirit. Avoid designing an investment strategy which creates a lifestyle where you only live to work. Remember it is your money and your life – you are in control of your destiny.

Real Estate

You may have seen real estate seminars promoted as being capable of making you instantly rich. They suggest the key to acquiring a secure future is to own a portfolio of property investments. These seminars are targeted at people who need to reduce their non tax-deductible personal debt levels, and not acquire more debt. For home owners, the best thing to do with excess cash flow is to make extra repayments on their home loan. If you are living from pay packet to pay packet, your principal focus should be the elimination of personal debt, loans and credit card debt first, then your mortgage.

Substantial numbers of investors purchase investment properties believing that, for just a few dollars a week from them, the Tax Department will be contributing towards payments on the investment property. The idea of using other people's money to invest has been around for a long time but today this is not without risk. The typical arrangement in Australia involves utilising the equity available on your home as a deposit on an investment property, borrowing the balance, and paying interest only on the loan. The investor then uses the rent along with some extra money to service the loan. The interest on the loan is tax-deductible and the arrangement is termed **negative gearing** if the rent is less than the interest paid on the loan. The cash flow of the investment is negative (e.g. a loss) each year while the investor profits from the capital gained from the property. If the property falls in value you have a greater loss than just the cumulative years of loss. If the property increases in value the gain is achieved in a more benign tax environment (e.g. subject to capital gains tax – 50 per cent of the taxpayer's marginal rate if the investment has been held for more than 12 months – as opposed to income tax). Most property investors have no idea whether their negatively geared properties actually make any profit, because they do not know how to do the calculations.

Let's consider this example:

> John purchased a unit in 1988 for $115,000 that had an **investment yield** (in rent) of $5750 or 5 per cent per annum. He borrowed the total purchase price including funds to cover the legal and the stamp duty costs. His total debt was $121,000. He paid interest only on the loan. From 1988 to 2000 his interest rate has averaged 8 per cent or $9680 per annum. He sold the unit in 2000 for $150,000. When you include his **net return** each year (that is, his income from the investment after all the expenses such as rates, interest, body corporate fees, repairs etc. have been paid), this makes a total 3 per cent net return before capital gains tax.

The complexities of geared investing require investors to understand that tax relief does not necessarily make a loss-making venture into a profitable venture. The critical component in using gearing is the total return (that is, the amount you make when you sell the property) in comparison to the cost of funds (that is, the amount you spent on maintaining the loan). As a rule, if a geared investment is unlikely to deliver double the rate of inflation in growth, then it is unlikely that your after-tax return will exceed inflation.

Other issues you need to consider:

- the lack of liquidity of property investment
- the high transaction costs in establishing and getting out of property in comparison to other investments
- the risk associated if your property is damaged, or if you are unable to find a tenant.

If you have a geared investment you should ensure you have:

- adequate life insurance and income protection insurance
- substantial cash reserves to protect you in the event of unemployment.

Many participants in the property industry accuse financial advisers (Certified Financial Planners) of a bias against property because of their reluctance to recommend direct property investments. Personally, Jonathan finds it very difficult to recommend direct property (except for wealthy individuals) because of the issues covered above. In particular the liquidity issue and the high cost of entry and exit fees, such as stamp duties and state taxes and agents' fees.

One way of overcoming the liquidity problems of property investment is to invest in a geared investment portfolio held as listed investments on the stock exchange. When you invest in a listed investment you are buying a share of a company, business, building or portfolio of buildings. Ownership of the asset is divided into thousands of shares, which makes the buying and selling of them easier than a direct investment, as the market is far more liquid – investments can be converted back to cash in 48 hours. If your share portfolio has been used as security for an investment loan, you can let the interest add to the principal amount owing as long as you have the capacity to borrow more funds from your margin lender. Many direct property investors are not familiar with the listed property trust sector which trades on the stock exchange. These investments are worthy of consideration as they produce a healthy income yield of 6.5–8.5 per cent p.a. and provide high levels of capital growth when the property market in general grows strongly. The other benefit is that you only need $5000 to get started.

Before investing into property you should consider the problems that may cause financial pain:

- What is inflation and the demand for property in selected area? Is it a new area with many vacant blocks of land for sale and an over-supply of new homes?
- If you are negatively gearing can you afford to pay for the property if you cannot get a person to rent the property? If you are still paying off your own home, over what period can you afford to pay for two mortgages?
- Do you have a reserve cash fund for damages caused to the property by uncaring tenants?
- Promoters for investing in real estate often say they have made large fortunes from real estate. Have you examined the time frame in which they made their fortunes? What was the rate of inflation when they started? The first home they bought could have gone from $8000 in 1975 to $100,000 by 1982. Will we ever see that rate of increase in such a short period again?
- Are these promoters connected to the development they are promoting? This is a conflict of interest because they benefit financially if you buy. If it's such a great investment why do they want others to invest when they could be making more money for themselves?
- If you negatively gear on a property do you have to pay a commission to the promoters to find you tenants or do you have to invest money into books, seminars etc. to learn how to make more money?

Always do your own research by reading local newspapers and finding out previous sale prices in the area you wish to invest in. Check the rental section of the local newspaper and find out rental prices in the area. If you are going to invest in an area you should go and see other properties for sale or rent in the neighbourhood and find out how long they have been on the market.

For most of us when we envisage ourselves owning a large portfolio of property we only think of the benefits of how:

- our property will increase in value over a short period of time
- the tenants will always pay on time and vacate without leaving any repairs to be done

- building managers will always act in the building and the owners' best interests
- guests will want to repeat visit our holiday/hotel unit due to great amenities, etc.
- party animals would never trash our holiday/hotel unit!

Real estate is a good investment if you have a **diversified investment** portfolio including a retirement account and the real estate investment is in a good location. We cannot emphasise enough the importance of conducting your own research and understanding what your losses may be if your property is not rented for long periods of time.

The attractions of borrowing to invest are obvious, but you really should consider the benefits of investing for positive cash flow, ensuring that you minimise your investment risk and protect your access to liquidity. See Chapter 3, Budgeting for the Investment Property Annual Expenses Table (pages 44–5).

Alternatives to Owning Property Directly

You don't have to own property directly, with all the attendant hassles of property management. You can invest in property using a range of **securitised** alternatives, such as listed and unlisted **property trusts**, or **property syndicates**. The difference with a securitised investment is that your money is pooled with other investors to purchase a range of investment grade properties. Syndicates, on the other hand, are smaller groups of investors who pool their funds to purchase a specific building or small portfolio of buildings.

The advantage for property trust investors is that they are able to purchase blue chip Central Business District property, have the building professionally managed and enjoy consistently good yields and growth prospects. Investors can choose between listed property trusts (traded on the stock exchange) or unlisted property trusts (run by fund managers who typically purchase the listed trusts). A major advantage is the liquidity offered by these investments. If you owned a factory unit and needed to buy a new car, you can't just sell one tenth of your factory, but in a listed trust you can sell 10 per cent of your shares any business day.

Property syndicates carry a higher level of risk as they lack the diversification of the listed and unlisted property trusts. Syndicates, however, offer investors direct exposure to the tax benefits such as depreciation. The downside to the property syndicate is that the investment term is typically 10 years, and redemptions are at the manager's discretion.

The Share Market

Investing in the share market can be the equivalent of either putting your money in the bank, or walking into a casino. Whether you are a gambler or an investor will determine the strategy you follow. The gambler will most likely be exposed to extraordinary fluctuations in portfolio value, whereas the investor will receive relatively consistent long-term income and investment growth. Outlined below are some basic rules about investing in stocks.

Before we look at the share market let's consider why it is a good place to invest your money. Shares usually offer the highest returns of any asset class over the longer term and have consistently outperformed bonds, property and **fixed interest investments**. Aside from the ability to usually offer the highest long-term returns of any asset class, investing in shares offers you the potential for future long-term capital growth, which helps to preserve the value of the portfolio against the eroding effects of inflation.

It is important that investors recognise that the share market reflects the performance of the economy. When people feel affluent and are investing in their futures or consuming goods and services, the profits drive share markets.

It is recognised that investment overseas may produce valuable benefits through portfolio diversification. The value of the Australian equity market represents less than 2 per cent of the value of the world equity markets. This suggests that investment opportunities beyond the domestic market are significant. International investing not only provides the diversification necessary to reduce risk but also is a means to achieve a higher return. Investing internationally has the potential advantages of giving:

- the ability to invest in industries not represented in the domestic market
- opportunities arising from economies at different points in their economic cycle
- opportunities arising from economies at different stages of economic development.

The primary considerations for domestic investors interested in undertaking overseas investment is risk diversification and performance maximisation.

When deciding how to buy shares, investors have two choices. They can invest directly and choose a portfolio of stocks or they can use a managed fund where a professional manager decides what to buy and sell. A managed fund pools your money with the money of thousands of other investors to form an investment fund. Specialist investment managers then invest the money in the fund on your behalf. Instead of having $2000 or even $20,000 to invest, your money has access to the investment buying power of millions of dollars. This buying power means you can take advantage of opportunities normally available to large corporations or those with extensive specialist knowledge.

Managed funds have a number of benefits such as:

- Providing you with diversification that in turn reduces your investment risk. You are able to invest in a number of companies for little cost.
- Giving you access to trained investment specialists who constantly research and monitor the investment markets to determine the best possible investment opportunities.
- Enabling you usually to access your funds within 10 days.

Managed funds are attractive for investments overseas, as the fund manager brings additional skills and information to the investment selection process that an individual may not be able to access. Fund managers also take care of the complexities of holding investments in a number of different countries.

If you decide to purchase shares directly, you should be aware that you are probably increasing your risk due to a lack of diversification. In order to reduce investment risk in your portfolio you should aim to hold a portfolio of not less than 12 stocks, and given the cost of brokerage, no individual hold should be less than $10,000.

Within a share portfolio you should also look to diversify between industry sectors owning stock in at least seven industry sectors. As you can see the process is not one that begins and ends with an opinion that a stock represents a good buy: the process needs structure and strategy, and most people (not all) are better suited to investing with the assistance of professional advice.

Rules:

- Never buy a stock because a friend, relative or acquaintance recommended it.
- Never buy a stock without knowing what it is.
- Never be talked into a stock by a broker if it varies from your fundamental stock selection strategy.
- If the return on investment sounds too good to be true, it probably is.

Investing in the stock market requires more than just picking a stock because you think it might do well. No one can predict whether the stock market will rise or fall. However, there are well educated individuals who have studied previous stock market fluctuations, and often have an inside view of how many companies are run. From these and other variables, these stock market experts can make educated assumptions about how a stock will perform.

You should recognise there are some instances where no level of education can predict stock market outcomes; for example, the bombing of the World Trade Center, which caused airline and insurance stocks to plummet.

To appreciate the skills required to invest in the stock market, Jonathan recommends you read the book *Reminiscences of a Stock Operator* by Edwin Lefevre, published by John Wiley & Sons Inc. If you're tempted to engage in speculation in either the stock, futures, or currency markets, Jonathan recommends *The Education of a Speculator* by Victor Niederhoffer, also published by John Wiley & Sons Inc.

Fixed Interest

Fixed interest refers to the asset class that includes government and corporate bonds, debentures, term deposits, insurance bonds and mortgage trusts. These investments are characterised by the predetermined income yield that the investment will provide. Fixed interest securities provide a predictable income and capital return, which can be matched to an investor's liabilities.

Fixed interest plays two very important roles. It:

- provides a consistent and reliable income flow
- has relatively low investment risk and volatility, and acts to reduce overall portfolio risk, at the expense of long-term capital growth.

As a consequence, care must be taken to balance the co-existing but contrasting goals of achieving a desirable income level, minimising risk and providing long-term growth. We believe this reiterates the need for a diversified and balanced approach to investment.

When investing in fixed interest, your investment goal should be carefully matched to the chosen investment. In most cases individual investors can do quite well, outperforming equivalent bank returns by utilising a fixed interest managed fund. The managed funds have sufficient volume of funds to purchase diversified portfolios of fixed interest investments across the **interest rate yield curve**.

Many investors mistake 'fixed interest' for 'risk free', but this is not the case. Fixed interest is a relatively low risk investment in comparison to other asset classes, but it does experience volatility in terms of the underlying investment value.

International Fixed Interest

International bonds in a portfolio provide diversification of interest rate risk across different markets, as each market will perform differently during any period of their economic cycle. To achieve maximum benefit from diversification and to take advantage of international economic cycles, an investment portfolio should include some international fixed interest exposure.

Investing internationally does present investors with risks that require consideration. One of the most important of these is foreign currency risk, and the need to continually manage this exposure. We would recommend that investors only gain international fixed interest exposure utilising a fund that hedges their currency risk. We would also not recommend high exposure to this asset class.

How to Design an Investment Portfolio

Designing an investment portfolio is a process that requires you to determine your:

- investment **time horizon**
- risk profile
- investment goals.

These three issues establish a set of parameters that any portfolio must meet. Your investment time horizon is an important guide to the level of exposure to growth investments (e.g. shares and property) in the portfolio. This needs to be looked at before selecting the optimal portfolio.

Most people end up with investment portfolios that contain inappropriate investments because they seemed like a good idea at the time. Most portfolios Jonathan sees don't have enough exposure to risk, or have been designed with too much risk. Some portfolios are under-diversified, or the client has not invested at all, accumulating cash and waiting for the next 1929-style stock market crash (which may never happen) to buy up some bargain priced stocks.

Creating Your Own Portfolio

We suggest you consider your time horizon and your general risk tolerance, as first order issues, and then identify an appropriate asset allocation.

For example, a 20-year-old's retirement fund should be invested into an aggressive portfolio with a 95 per cent allocation to growth assets of shares and property, with 5 per cent allocated to cash and fixed interest.

Compare this asset allocation to a retiree who has a need for retirement funds to generate reliable income and have his/her capital keep up with inflation. In this case you might have an allocation of 37.5 per cent in income producing investments, such as fixed interest and cash, with 62.5 per cent invested in shares and property.

Finally, the difference between a mediocre and a great investor comes down to education, choice and diversification. Ensure you always understand your risk profile (high/low) and your time frame, and seek professional financial advice before you implement any investment strategy. The initial cost of a suitable investment strategy is worth paying to reduce the risk involved when selecting asset classes you may not understand. Ultimately you want the goal of growth and financial security for yourself and your family.

Investing for Your Children

Selecting appropriate investments for your children's future is never an easy task. Take into consideration the purpose of the investment and the tax implications associated with your choice. Some governments offer tax concessions for children's accounts. However, the Australian government levies punitive tax on children's unearned income at 47 per cent, making children the highest taxed group in Australian society. The Australian government is planning to offer parents tax incentives to place money into retirement funds for their children's future. Other options available to parents are outlined below.

Managed Funds

A managed fund is a fund which consists of the pooled money of many investors managed by a fund manager. The fund uses this money to invest in a wide spectrum of investment options. This option allows you to contribute as little as $100 per month with some funds. Managed funds are not particularly tax effective but are still a good option worth considering. The advantage of using managed funds is that small investors are gaining exposure to diversification that they could not otherwise achieve.

Shares

Shares are a great option as long as you invest in quality blue chip stocks. It is always recommended that you seek professional advice, as your portfolio should be diversified. Another option is to purchase shares in a listed investment company.

Scholarship Funds

Scholarship funds are a great investment alternative for your children's education as long as they progress to the tertiary level. The down side to this investment is that you only receive return of capital and no earnings, if your children don't go on to university.

Retirement Funds

In Australia, the government is considering tax incentives for parents to invest in their children's retirement. While you may derive a tax break from this investment we would not recommend it. Your children's retirement is not really an issue you should worry about. It is more important to ensure your children have funds to assist in the payment for further education or other options early in their adult lives. Waiting to receive funds in your mid to late 60s is a long way off when you are in your 20s.

Insurance Bonds

Insurance bonds are an investment with a life insurance company. The life insurance company pays tax on the investment earnings and if you hold the investment for longer than 10 years you receive the proceeds tax paid. Insurance bonds are a great option as they are tax effective.

Traded Endowment Policies

Traded endowment policies (TEPs) are insurance policies purchased by investors before maturity. TEPs offer investors a partly guaranteed rate of return and a known maturity value at a specific date in the future. TEPs are also subject to the same tax treatment as insurance bonds. The advantage for parents is that they can invest now, knowing with some confidence how much they will receive on the TEPs' maturity.

TEPs are an excellent option for education funding.

Maria and Herman

Maria and Herman had three children and decided they would put aside some money every week for their children until they reached 21. Maria and Herman had planned that the money saved would be used for further education but did not want to restrict their investments by placing them into a scholarship fund, opting instead to invest in a managed fund. As each child reached the age of 21 they received $40,000, which was to be spent on university/college fees. Only one of Maria and Herman's children went on to obtain a university degree. He used his money to pay off part of his education debt. The other two children also received their $40,000 and both used it to purchase property. Of the three children the one who went on to further education now earns double the income of his siblings. He achieved the goal of education for which the money was saved.

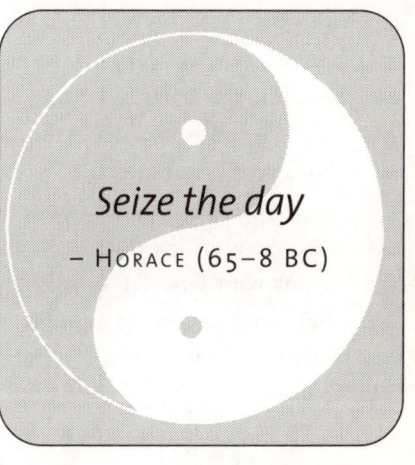

Seize the day
– HORACE (65–8 BC)

Had Maria and Herman placed their money into a scholarship fund, they would have received only their capital back with no earnings. It was by chance that they selected an investment option. This not only grew in value but helped their children with their individual goals at age 21. However, before you invest any money for your children, remember that while you may wish for your children to go on to further education, it does not mean it will happen. Be realistic and don't make investment choices that are restrictive.

Wills and Estate Planning

Have you ever discussed any details of how you would like your estate distributed? Will and estate planning is often a neglected area when organising your financial affairs. We can never be sure when our last day on this earth may be, but we can certainly ensure our will and estate details are in order and stored in a secure place for our family members. Within the balanced framework of Money Karma this responsibility must be addressed to ensure all our loved ones have been considered in the event of our death.

If you have children under 18 years old and both you and your partner were to die, does any other family member know how you would want your children cared for or educated? Children under 18 years of age need continued support and guidance. You need to ensure there is adequate and appropriate planning for all needs of your dependants in the event of the death of both parents /guardians.

If you own a home and have savings, you need to consider setting up a trust that will ensure the sale of your assets is used for the education and care of your dependants. If you have personal items you wish kept for your children when they reach adulthood, make a detailed list of which items are to be sold and which to be kept. If you neglect to adequately plan your will, your home will be sold and your personal effects may end up going at auction and the choices are decided by others.

You also need to select who will be your dependants' legal guardian. This is a crucial role, as this person will take responsibility for the love and care of your family.

The continued care of your pets must also be planned. You need to decide if they will be given to a loving home, the RSPCA or you'd prefer they be put to rest in the event of your death.

Adults should all have a legal will. It is important to allow for the orderly distribution of your assets and also gives direction in respect of your burial or cremation. If you have dependants, remember you need to nominate who should become their legal guardian. If you have financial dependants it is important you have a will professionally drafted. An ambiguous will could erode your estate and cause family conflict. Legal disputes arising from an estate are paid for by the estate. Often it is the lawyers who benefit most from an estate in the event of a dispute. Not all assets will form part of your estate: for example, assets owned by joint tenants become the property of the surviving party following a death. Also, a beneficial interest in a trust does not form part of an estate as trusts are entities in their own right and the trust deed will determine the appropriate beneficiary.

This is a brief summary of some of the issues involved in estate planning. You should regularly update and revise your will as circumstances change. We emphasise again that, it is essential you obtain legal advice when organising your will and estate planning.

Life and Income Protection Insurance

If you were to have a fatal accident or lose your job tomorrow, could your partner or family continue to live in their usual style? Appropriate life and income protection insurance is a vital component of any financial plan. It offers the family security against the prospect of financial hardship in the event of an accident or death.

In order to determine the appropriate amount of life and income protection insurance, it is important to know how much cover (if any) is provided by the employer and the conditions associated with that insurance cover. You may need to talk to your employer to establish this information. Make yourself familiar with all your work entitlements and conditions.

Ensure you have adequate life insurance to cover your debts and provide your dependants with sufficient capital to continue living at a comfortable standard. Irrespective of the incomes of partners in your household, plan for both parties to have enough life insurance cover to pay off all household debts. Remember that a high-income earner may need sufficient cover on a low-income spouse to pay for home help or childcare in the event of that person's illness or death. Alternatively it could take a non-working spouse some time to retrain for the workforce in the event of the high-income person's illness or death (and they may also require home help or childcare if returning to work).

In determining what is an appropriate level of death cover, consider the full implications for your family in this eventuality.

Income Protection Insurance provides for the payment of up to 75 per cent of your salary if you are unable to work in your normal occupation. Policy conditions usually impose a waiting period of between 14 and 180 days. Usually the longer the specified waiting period, the lower the premium cost.

Summary

- Always understand what your investments are.
- When selecting a Certified Financial Planner (CFP) ensure you feel they are trustworthy and that they can demonstrate a depth of thinking with strategy options.
- Be a proactive investor and not a reactive one, when your investment is affected by adverse financial conditions.
- Understand how fluctuations in the marketplace may affect your investment.
- Manage investment risk by holding a portfolio including a variety of asset classes.
- When investing, diversification is key.
- Diversification protects investors from the total failure of an individual investment.
- Investment choices impact on your lifestyle.
- Control your own destiny.
- Refrain from purchasing stocks because a friend, relative, or acquaintance recommends it.
- Don't be talked into a stock by a broker if it varies from your fundamental stock selection strategy.
- The difference between a mediocre and a great investor is the difference between education, choice and diversification.
- Understand your risk profile (high/low) and your time frame, and seek professional advice before you implement any investment strategy.
- An investor's goal is to generate growth and financial security.
- Ensure you have a will and that it is up to date and stored securely.
- An ambiguous will could erode your estate and cause family conflict.
- Not all assets will form part of your estate: for example, assets owned by joint tenants become the property of the surviving party following a death.
- Always ensure you have adequate income protection and life insurance for the financial security of your family in the event of your death.

8

Ethical Investing

*There's an old saying which goes:
Once the last tree is cut and the last river poisoned,
you will find you cannot eat your money.*

– Joyce McLean (*The Globe and Mail*, 1989)

> *Labour to keep alive in your breast that little spark of celestial fire, called conscience.*
>
> — GEORGE WASHINGTON (1732–99)

Part of the journey to our financial destiny requires us to examine the way we live and interact within our community. Every decision we make has an effect on the development of our neighbourhoods, and the quality of life we create for our families, friends and community members. We must create an environment that allows us to lead a life that caters for all our needs and to examine how the choices we make with our money affect other elements in our world. We are talking about ethical investment and the consequences of ignoring or not understanding the impact of investment strategies on the enviroment. **Socially responsible investing** (SRI) is a term defined as the integration of an individual's investment objectives with his/her commitment to social concerns such as social justice, economic development, peace or a healthy environment (source: UK Social Investment Forum).

Today a growing number of shareholders are no longer passive investors. They actively take a proactive position on what the companies they invest in do with their money. Many shareholders don't want simply profit at any cost, but ensure that before investing in any stock, they have a full understanding of how a company operates, what effect it has on the environment, and how that company performs as a corporate citizen.

Investing ethically is no longer a niche market: SRI is becoming a popular choice for many investors. Many organisations and companies throughout the world understand there is an expectation that while financial objectives must be met, social and environmental responsibilities must not be ignored. Many so-called 'old economy' companies are moving towards becoming more socially responsible. This is a direct consequence of individual and institutional investors applying pressure, demanding information about the environmental impact of business activity, the openness and accountability of corporate governance and the company's involvement in business activities they deem unacceptable, such as weapons manufacturing or uranium mining.

In developing an ethical investment strategy the first step for the investor is to have a clear understanding of your personal social priorities. It may be difficult to meet your specific ethical agenda by using one or more of the available ethical investment funds, promoted by fund managers. Using an ethical investment fund might seem an easy solution, but it may involve compromise with regard to some issues. For example, you may object to investing in companies that clear timber. A company involved in forestry and woodchip export might pass a fund manager's screen on the basis that it is involved in timber plantations (meeting a sustainability test) and rehabilitates the forests that have been exploited (meeting an environmentally friendly test, for example has no convictions for breach of environmental laws).

Deciding to invest ethically and discovering your personal social priorities are just the beginning. Those with sufficient funds can build their own portfolio with assistance from their investment adviser. It is important to begin with the same investment criteria to which a non-ethical portfolio would be subject. First, screen a universe of investments, and then apply your socially responsive screens in order to end up with an investment portfolio that satisfies your personal social priorities.

Some fund managers build portfolios based on a specific criterion, which determines a company's approval for SRI. Often companies are excluded from the SRI rating because they derive revenue from weapons, gambling, alcohol, tobacco, birth control, or activities that involve environmental destruction, human rights abuses, poor labour practices, animal rights abuses or abortion.

The push for ethical investment strategies is also an area that **superannuation** (retirement fund) trustees are beginning to examine, as fund members become more aware of the social and environmental unsustainability of some funds. A hindrance to SRI funds being recommended by professional analysts has been the lack of **wholesale investment options**, combined with a lack of independent research on fund manager processes and corporate capacity. Another stumbling block has been the overexposure of SRI funds to the technology and financial services sectors, which doesn't fit the highly disciplined approach that many professional analysts follow in constructing portfolios.

Jonathan recently had a client who was interested in SRI. Jonathan constructed a portfolio that met his company's requirements in terms of

15 stocks, across seven industry sectors, with no single stock representing more than double its **index weighting**. Then he and his firm went through a process of eliminating those stocks that failed the SRI tests that they believed the client would apply. What they found was that no independent research existed on the individual companies. After they culled the portfolio they went through the portfolio building process again to ensure they had 15 recommended stocks. They learnt that it is difficult to have a balanced SRI with investments across seven industry sectors, and not end up with a portfolio overweighted in the finance and technology sectors.

Since this experience they have engaged a consultant to undertake the necessary research on companies that meet our initial investment screening process. After negotiating with the client we have decided to invest across a range of sectors that meets our professional standards, as well as our client's personal criteria for ethical investments.

SRI still remains a relatively small sector and this is due to the limited knowledge of and/or lack of demand for SRI funds. Consumers interested in SRI need to discuss the options available with their financial advisers or stockbrokers.

Money Karma and Ethics

The purpose of Money Karma is to develop a quality of life that creates balance, harmony and happiness within all areas of your life. We need to understand how ethics play an important role in the way we communicate and exist on this planet. You create your own experiences. If you lead a life based entirely on self-interest, and do not take into account the effects you may have on others around you, then that is the world you will exist in. The saying 'what goes around comes around' is an effective metaphor. If you treat other human beings as though they are without feelings or emotions then this is how others will treat you. The other side of this equation is that if you are a compassionate person who takes other people's feelings into consideration then this is the world you will live in.

Many people don't practise ethical behaviour. They live their lives fulfilling their latest desire and wallowing in a state of selfishness and self-pity. If we allow ourselves to continually engage life in this way, without contributing to the growth of our own and others' quality of life, we are not really experiencing life to the full. A truly fulfilled existence includes being sincere and ethical as part of your everyday life.

No matter what our circumstances, we need to adopt strategies that will make us more empowered individuals with control over our own lives. Whatever we do to the world or to others we also do to ourselves – it is a continually evolving partnership.

Investing ethically is not limited to investing in the stock market. It is also about the way you choose to live, spend and save. We all have choices and these choices impact upon our environment and the quality of air, water and land we live from.

To fully appreciate Money Karma we must have a holistic approach to every human and living thing. We must develop an awareness of the effect our possessions and foods have on our environment, including the effects of chemicals, genetically modified foods, the fuels we use (coal, oil, gas, wood) and the type of motor vehicle we purchase. For example, we can make conscious decisions to use as little energy as possible in an effort to limit the effects of excess greenhouse gases on our earth.

An important point to consider is the type and size of motor vehicle

> *The only freedom which deserves the name, is that of pursuing our own good in our own way, so long as we do not attempt to deprive others of theirs, or impede their efforts to obtain it.*
>
> – JOHN STUART MILL (1806–73)

> *We are living beyond our means. As a people we have developed a lifestyle that is draining the earth of its priceless and irreplaceable resources without regard for the future of our children and people around the world.*
>
> – MARGARET MEAD (1901–78)

you choose. The larger the car, the greater the cost of fuel, servicing, insurance and repayments; but the impact is not only on your budget, it's also on air pollution and the planet.

Money Karma is not about making judgements on people or their possessions, but about understanding how your decisions will impact upon the earth and its diminishing resources. We should all aim to have less impact on the environment, as far as possible leaving the earth as we found it for the future generations. We have inherited an earth already suffering from the logging of forests and pollution of waterways by past generations.

Here are some examples where there is an impact on both our budgets and our environment:

- Supermarkets leave refrigerator and freezer doors open and waste energy. The cost of running them is passed on to the consumer through higher priced goods. Would you leave your refrigerator door open 24 hours a day at home?
- Department and specialty stores use airconditioning or heating without keeping entry doors closed. Once again, this cost is passed onto the consumer. Would you cool or heat your home leaving all your doors open? It is not just the consumer who pays for this waste of energy, but the entire planet, as it contributes to global warming.
- Many government and corporate buildings leave all their office lights on 24 hours a day. Security is often used as an excuse for this waste of energy. These buildings could simply use sensor lighting.
- Governments use our tax dollars to extend road systems instead of improving public transport options first.
- Public and private swimming pools are still being heated with gas or electricity and not covered at night to retain heat. Solar heating and solar blankets are an option that cost very little to maintain.
- Commuters often use cars with only one occupant instead of car-pooling. Sharing fuel costs, tolls and parking fees would make a major saving on our budgets. Often we are forced to use our motor vehicles because of inadequate and unaffordable public transport options.

A recent survey conducted in several Australian metropolitan cities found that wealthier people had a higher probability of using public transport. Lower income workers rarely used public transport, placing greater pressure on their budgets. This study found that wealthier people often lived closer to CBDs and had greater access to public transport. These wealthy commuters often didn't own motor vehicles, opting to put their money into a more expensive inner city home.

Environmentalists such as David Suzuki and organisations such as Greenpeace have been publicising the environmental and financial costs of decisions we make about the way we live.

> *As man proceeds towards his announced goal of the conquest of nature, he has written a depressing record of destruction, directed not only against the earth he inhabits but against the life that shares it with him.*
>
> – RACHEL CARSON (1907–64)

- Governments pass legislation making consumers pay higher tariffs on smaller cars (which are fuel-efficient) and lower tariffs on large cars. (Even so, purchasing a large car is false economy because the cost of fuel and other running costs end up being substantially higher.) Often, tariffs are set this way in an effort to win votes.
- Some goods are highly packaged. Packaging is a major cost to most producers and you pay extra for these heavily wrapped goods, while the waste may contribute to litter and landfill. The extra cost of buying highly packaged goods has a major impact on your budget.
- Increased farming and consumption of meat adds to pollution on our earth. Livestock produce carbon dioxide and methane, which are greenhouse gases. Large areas of the earth's wilderness have been cleared to make way for farms. Excess consumption of animal products (meat, milk, eggs and cheese) can contribute to health problems such as heart disease and obesity. Also, these products are often the most expensive items in your food budget.
- We frequently purchase goods and products that are not locally produced. The further a product has to travel, the more energy is consumed and the cost of this not only adds to your budget but also adds to the further pollution of the earth.
- Do you use as much clean water as you want (because you can pay for it) without understanding it is a finite resource?

> *I have never found in a long experience of politics that criticism is ever inhibited by ignorance.*
>
> HAROLD MACMILLAN (1894–1986)

There is a correlation between how we live and how we spend. Choosing to ignore the impact our living standards are having on this planet is selfish. It is important to remember that it is the industrialised countries that have caused the greatest impact on our planet over the last 150 years due to fossil fuel usage. We are part of this over-use.

Australia is leading the world in the development of green energy technology, including solar and water power. Yet it has shown reluctance to commit to reducing greenhouse emissions, and is falling behind Europe and the UK in the provision of public transport. It is up to us to ensure these energy-efficient alternatives are further developed and implemented. California, amongst other places, is already living with energy blackouts and is paying higher rates for fossil fuel electricity consumption.

We believe that you should value every cent you earn and spend it wisely. You only live once, so stand up for your beliefs and be quietly heard. Have a sense of purpose by being informed about party politics when you vote, and by writing or emailing your opinions to politicians. You can see the chain effect between your actions and the results.

> *Global temperatures are going to rise faster this century than over the last 10,000 years*
>
> — GREENPEACE

Third-world people are not getting their fair share of what life has to offer. In our opinion, life is about connecting and sharing with others the standard of living we enjoy. With many people suffering in the world, it is obvious something is going wrong with our lifestyle choices, and we must accept some responsibility for it. Let's ensure future generations have clean air, water and forests. Today some social commentators and government officials make it seem unacceptable to appear to care for the earth and to be an environmentalist. If you cannot see that overuse of our earth's resources will have an impact on how you live and save, then it is just a matter of time.

Summary

- Create an environment that allows you to lead a life that caters for all your needs and to examine the choices you make with your money and how it affects other elements in our world.
- Companies throughout the world are increasingly expected to be socially and environmentally responsible and still maintain profitable financial objectives.
- When developing an ethical investment strategy, the first step is to have a clear understanding of your personal social priorities.
- Investors with sufficient funds can build their own SRI portfolio with assistance from their financial adviser.
- Companies are excluded from the SRI rating because they derive revenue from gambling, alcohol, tobacco, birth-control, or activities that involve environmental destruction, human rights abuses, poor labour practices, animal rights abuses or abortion.
- A truly fulfilling life is one lived in an ethical and sincere manner.
- Investing ethically is not limited to investing in the stock market. It is concerned with the way you choose to live, spend and save.
- Living ethically is not about making judgements on other people or their possessions; it is about understanding how your decisions will impact upon the earth and its diminishing resources.

Women and Finance

To have made a beginning is half of the business; dare to be wise.

– Horace (65–8 BC)

> *Pennies do not come from heaven. They have to be earned here on earth.*
> — MARGARET THATCHER

In this chapter we examine some issues faced by women in becoming financially independent and secure. In the 21st century, women still face many obstacles they need to overcome to achieve financial independence. Surveys indicate many women feel threatened whenever money is discussed. To achieve financial self-sufficiency, women need to take a more proactive stance on decisions that concern their lives and financial planning. They need to explore coping strategies for the future to ensure they are not burdened by debt or poverty later in life.

For some women extreme debt and poverty are major threats to their future financial security. These threats are not limited to women of the third world or to only specific socio-economic groups. Many women from western democratic nations also live with the hardships brought on by lack of financial security.

From the security of our comfortable western lifestyles, many women ignore or neglect to examine the ways in which they live and spend. Women need to ensure their main goal is self-sufficiency, whether they are married, in a de facto relationship or single. For many, raising children, working, establishing careers, studying, exercising and/or maintaining homes fills most of their day. This daily activity should not be used as an excuse to neglect financial planning for the future.

> *On average, in developed countries women earn 23 per cent less than men. In developing countries they earn 27 per cent less.*
> — WORLD BANK 2000

You may have read the above statistics and thought that you could not be classified as one of the women who may face financial hardship later in life. Even with a good education, and coming from a middle to upper class background, poverty or extreme financial hardship is something you need to consider. We urge you to examine some aspects of how well you are planning for your future. Listed below are some questions, which will assist you to assess whether you need to become more financially aware of your future.

> *Be not afraid of growing slowly. Be afraid only of standing still.*
>
> – CHINESE PROVERB

The Financial Wake-Up Call

- If you are working, do you know how much superannuation (retirement income) money you will need in retirement to maintain your current lifestyle?
- How much do you pay into superannuation retirement plan? How much is currently invested in your name?
- If you are married or in a de facto relationship and your relationship ends, would you be able to fund your current lifestyle?
- If you are a non-working spouse, do you have a superannuation retirement plan? If the answer is no, what funds would you have if your partner died or divorced you? What taxes would you need to pay from this sum?
- What skills do you have that could assist you to return to the workforce or to improve your current employment situation?
- If your partner or spouse became disabled and could no longer work, would you be able to support the family?
- Do you spend within a planned financial budget?
- Do you have a financial plan for your retirement?
- Do you know your risk tolerance levels when it comes to investing?
- What are your future goals?
- How much money do you think/know you will need to live comfortably in retirement?
- How much of your current income will you need in retirement?
- What are your current savings? Do you save on a regular basis?

- What are your current debts? Do you have a plan to pay these debts in a specific time frame?
- What do you spend weekly?
- Do you own your own home or pay a mortgage/rent? Is this property in your name or in joint names? Is there any property in your name? What is the ratio of debt to mortgage on property? If you rent, are you going to buy a home? Do you know if you should rent or buy?
- If you want a family, know how much it will cost you to raise a child. If you have children, do you have a budget for their education? Are your choices for your children realistic or will they impact on your retirement plan?

If you have no idea how much money you currently have or need in retirement, now is the time to become proactive. The worst thing is to ignore the reality of what your financial future will be. You need to consider that as our population ages and the number of younger workers decreases so does the revenue derived from taxation. There will be less government assistance available to cope with the demands of an ageing population and as we age the time left to save for retirement diminishes. Start a savings plan early to ensure a comfortable retirement.

A Woman's Reality

One reason why some women have less in retirement savings compared to men is the time women spend out of the workforce. Some women spend more than 10 years out of the workforce compared with just over one year for men. During this time out of the workforce women may have children, care for an elderly or unwell relative or they may go back to school to upgrade their skills. Therefore in this period these women are not contributing to any form of retirement plan. A reduced period of time in the workforce means some women may not be able to work long enough to fund their retirement. In this case they will need to be totally reliant upon their spouse's/partner's retirement savings. Another contributing factor is the level of jobs filled by women in the workplace. Women often hold casual or part-time jobs, which do not offer the same working conditions as full-time employment, for example annual paid leave, medical/sick days, health benefits or retirement contributions paid by employers for superannuation policies or other retirement programs.

Another contributing factor is that some women fail to generate comparable incomes to men due to employment opportunities. Many couples and families move interstate or overseas for their spouse or partner's job. Sometimes when skilled and unskilled women and their families relocate, they are unable to find suitable employment in their area of expertise. This also contributes to disrupted career paths for women, as they are never anywhere long enough to establish their career. It is advisable to always consider the benefits and disadvantages of moving (if you have a choice) to an area where you may be placing your career on hold.

Never assume you will be able to find work because, until you have looked, nothing is certain. It may be wise to ensure you have a job to go to before you move so that you are not placing your career, and most of all your financial future, at risk. This can also contribute to relationship issues as feelings of resentment towards the working spouse cause many problems. Ask yourself if your spouse would risk his career path by following you to a new location without a secured job. Is the promotion or extra income for your partner worth the stress and feelings of inequality if you cannot find work and you remain financially dependent? If you have a specialised field of expertise then any job will not suffice. You must be able to continue working towards the career you have trained for to ensure personal and job satisfaction.

Renee

Renee and her husband Blake had one child and lived in a large city where employment opportunities were abundant. He worked in the engineering industry and she in horticulture. Renee's husband was offered a job in a regional city, which meant an increase for his overall income. Renee and Blake did some initial research and found that employment opportunities for her would not be hard to find. Renee was tertiary educated and had worked in her industry for over 10 years. The couple moved interstate and settled into their new home and Renee started looking for work. They both loved living in this new city until weeks turned into months and Renee was still unable to find any employment. Her husband found his new job interesting but found the stress of his wife's unemployment detracted from the quality of life they had moved for. She started to resent her husband and felt that she had been placed in a role that made her totally reliant upon her husband for financial and emotional support. This was something that had never been a factor in their relationship before. Renee found that the group of friends she had met gave only limited support and did not totally relate to her unemployment problem. Renee had always lived and worked in an environment where women worked, raised children, went to school part/full-time and cared for their families as part of their daily routine.

Until you live somewhere you never know how easy or hard it will be to establish yourself. The reason Blake found employment was he had been recruited from interstate and his expertise was mandatory in his field, so only qualified professionals could be employed. The couple moved back to their original city, and Renee had to once again search for employment and re-establish herself in her field. The cost for her included not only the lost income and retirement income contributions, but it also affected her emotionally as she realised how important it is to be independent and self-supportive. Her husband moved back into a position that was equivalent to the job he had left. Renee was not so lucky as her time out of the workforce had worked against her.

Education and Women

One of the main reasons some women face financial hardship at some point in their lives is their relative lack of education. In most cases your earning capacity and ability to accumulate wealth are directly related to your level of education. With more education you have a greater capacity to acquire assets such as retirement savings, homes and other investments. More education also means there may be fewer candidates competing for employment at your level. Any advantage you can give yourself to make your life financially secure is worth the effort. For most people in the workforce it means learning to study and work. If you are a parent of daughters, it is important you give them every opportunity to gain as much education as possible. This does not mean you need to fund it all yourself, but you can make sure they value education and make every effort to be the best they can. The greatest gift you can give your child is the foundation of a good education and the ability to use problem solving on the many obstacles of life.

> *A mother is not a person to lean on but a person to make leaning unnecessary.*
> — DOROTHY CANFIELD FISHER (1879–1958)

Awaiting the Knight in Shining Armour

Some women believe that somewhere there is a man prepared to take care of them and all the responsibilities of daily life. These women believe their ideal man will ensure they are secure, and they will not have to be financially responsible or accountable for any aspects of their life, including calculating the family budget, saving or retirement planning. This is a myth and it shows that these women are not living in reality. Don't be afraid to educate yourself in the skills required for responsible financial planning.

Two examples below highlight that some women, whether professional or not, still perpetuate the Cinderella Syndrome.

Sophia

Sophia is an extremely successful woman who became a multimillionaire by working her way up the corporate ladder to become one of the leaders in her industry. During her early working career she met and fell in love with Steve, a man who was not associated with her career. He was five years older and made her feel happy and complete. Sophia felt guilty that she earned substantially more than her partner. Her long hours also contributed to these feelings of guilt as he was forced to spend much of his time alone or with friends. Sophia was never very effective at managing her money. Steve suggested he could manage her money and she was more than happy to allow him to do so. Gradually he spent less time at his work and eventually quit his job, opting to make a career of managing Sophia's money. Steve thought if he invested her money into stocks and other investments he could generate more income. He lost vast sums of money by making bad investment decisions and never disclosed the losses to her. Sophia neglected to enquire about any aspect of her financial situation. After 15 years their standard of living remained unchanged so Sophia was unaware of their financial situation until their relationship deteriorated and they separated. She instructed him to divide their money equally. This was when he informed her that her finances were depleted due to his poor investment choices. Sophia was now aware that she had allowed herself to be placed in this situation. She had believed she needed a man to look after the finances. It was a painful lesson after a long and successful career and today she is responsible for her own financial management.

Carmen

Carmen, a woman in her early 60s, is divorced and has two daughters who live out of town. She currently lives on her own in a middle class suburb paying off a townhouse on which she owes more than 50 per cent. She has no formal qualifications other than a secretarial diploma. Currently she supports herself by working part-time as a childcarer for an agency. Carmen neglected to save for her retirement. She recently devised a plan which she believes will ensure her a secure retirement in her old age. Her plan is save enough money for a trip to Italy where she hopes she will meet a wealthy old bachelor or widower who will marry her. She plans to live in her future husband's Italian villa for six months of the year and then live the other six months in her townhouse. Carmen is really serious and resolute when she tells you her plan. She has already saved some of her airfare to Europe.

What these women and others who avoid financial issues are really demonstrating is fear of their financial situation. They are scared to take on financial responsibility without any guidance or reassurance that they are making the right financial decisions. It is hard to imagine that women who have capably raised children, maintained homes, worked, and developed careers are fearful when faced with organising and implementing financial strategies for themselves and their family. If you fear discussing finances, consider the following questions:

- What financial decisions are you responsible for in your relationship? (Other than going to the grocery store and buying goods for the home.)

- Do you do any of the banking? (Paying the mortgage/rent, allocating funds into your savings/retirement account or paying off other loans/debts.) Is it done automatically and deducted from your or your partner's weekly income?
- Have you attempted to do Internet banking? Have you ever paid bills over the phone?
- Have you ever paid your credit card, telephone, electricity or other bills?
- Have you ever applied for a credit card, mortgage, or new bank account on your own? Do you know what the process involves?
- Have you ever considered organising a retirement savings plan? Do you have one for yourself? Do you know how much money you will need to live on in retirement? If you have a partner, do they have a retirement plan? Will their income be enough for you both to live on? Have you discussed this issue with a financial adviser?
- Do you know how much money there is in your bank accounts?
- Do you know what financial debts/liabilities you currently have?
- Do you have a budget?
- Do you spend without a plan?
- Where is your family's net worth held? Is it in your family home?
- Do you know the importance of having a diversified financial portfolio?
- Do you lack control over your spending and is this a reason to avoid paying the bills?
- Is spending more than you earn part of your financial fear?

If you have looked at these questions and discovered you have little or no responsibility when it comes to your family budget, then you need to address this issue immediately. If for some reason your partner or spouse is in an accident, suddenly becomes ill, dies or leaves you, it is important that you are not burdened with financial hardships due to a lack of money management experience. If you do have a financial phobia this is your opportunity to challenge yourself and to start taking some responsibility. Once you begin to overcome your financial fears the rest gets easier. Women are great problem solvers and by having an equal input into your finances you may find you have some innovative ideas that could improve the way your family is currently managing its finances.

To begin overcoming your financial fears, discuss your financial situation with your spouse/partner and decide what your plans are going to be.

- What financial strategies are in place (if any) and why have they been selected?
- How are your weekly/monthly expenses calculated and what budget is in place to ensure all of your liabilities are being met?
- Are there realistic goals, each with deadlines set?
- What retirement planning is in place for each of you?
- Do you have a realistic target of how much retirement income you both need to live on later in life? (See Chapter 11, Baby Boomers' Financial Awakening for Estimated Retirement Living Costs chart, page 178.) Even if you are only in your late 20s you need to start planning for your retirement soon, as our world and employment opportunities constantly change. Many of us will face redundancies, have several careers/jobs, periods of unemployment and may need time out of work for illness or childcare.

> *I hope there will come a day when you, daughter mine, or your daughter, can truly say 'I'm not a feminist. I'm a person.'*
>
> – BETTY FRIEDAN

You should ensure you have a detailed list of your current net worth including any liabilities you may have incurred. Many of us assume we are financially worth a lot more than we really are and live in a state of financial delusion. With this delusion people live with unrealistic budgets that they cannot maintain long term and they will be forced to make drastic lifestyle changes later in life.

With this knowledge, you now have all of the financial information you need to ensure successful money management strategies can be discussed with a professional Financial Adviser. To fully adopt **Money Karma** into your life it is imperative that you balance all areas within your life. This means taking responsibility for all areas and not allowing excuses to deter you from your financial pathway and destiny.

Divorce, Retirement and Investing

Many women remain unaware of the impact their retirement is going to have on them financially. To retire comfortably you need to take an active role in planning for the financial security of your retirement. Planning for your future means considering all aspects of your life and being consciously aware of the risk of issues you may have to deal with. No one ever wants to plan for divorce and everyone believes it will never happen to their relationship. However the reality is that in Australia almost 50 per cent of marriages end in divorce. This means close to one out of every two marriages is going to end in divorce.

An Australian Bureau of Statistics study has found that 8 per cent of marriages break down within five years of marriage, 19 per cent within ten years, 32 per cent within 20 years and 39 per cent within thirty years. The tragic part of these statistics is that the older we are, the less likely we will be in paid employment and many women are dependent on their spouse's or partner's retirement income.

For some couples, drawn-out legal battles between divorcing partners who cannot reach a suitable settlement mean the amount of money left to share is reduced. This is one aspect of divorce which creates severe financial hardship for both parties.

In Australia, legislation has been passed which allows divorcing couples to include superannuation (retirement benefits) as part of the assets test to be divided in a divorce settlement. While this legislation will assist those with little or no superannuation savings (often women), the fact that this money is locked away until you reach 65 means you have to find alternative means of surviving and re-establishing yourself until you can access this asset. Dividing the equity in a home or other assets between two parties also means financial hardship may be an issue for both parties.

The economic reality for divorcing women is often related to their employment prospects. Many who have children will be faced with the problems of organising safe, affordable childcare, flexible working hours and suitable housing. For those with limited education, obtaining flexible working conditions translates into part-time/casual, low paying

> Two thirds of all poor adults living in the USA are women. One out of every four children in the USA lives in a poor family.
> – EQUAL RIGHTS ADVOCATES ORGANISATION

jobs, often with no provision for retirement plans. Some of these women will be challenged with the reality of the 'living wage'.

Even if you are happily married or in a de facto relationship you should always ensure you have made every effort to plan, save and/or work for your own retirement. Having children and raising/caring for a family is a wonderful contribution to make to our community, but you should understand the risk you are taking if you actively choose never to return to the workforce or to upgrade your skills.

Many women have children, work full-time and some even study part/full-time. This not only contributes to their own mental wellbeing but it serves as a good role model for your children.

> The unpalatable truth is that a substantial proportion of women still accept the sexual division of labour which sees home-making as women's principal activity and income earning as men's principal activity in life.
> – CATHERINE HARKIM (*The Observer Review*, 1996)

As a woman living in today's society it is time to start taking on an outlook that ensures you are self-sufficient and able to be self-supportive. Stepping out of your comfort zone and challenging yourself is never an easy task. It is essential that you don't suffer through the hardships of low-paying career prospects and a diminishing lifestyle. If you can see this happening to you, what is deterring you from returning to school and achieving the qualifications you require for your chosen career? Everything you achieve is for yourself. When you really value yourself your financial security is paramount.

It's important to note that the majority of divorced women end up as sole carers for their children, in some cases without any financial support from their former spouse or partner. When deciding whether to have children, it is wise to assess your earning capability. If you are left as a sole carer for your children you may be their only means of financial support. Never allow yourself to be placed in the situation where you have children but no ability to care for and financially support them on your own.

For some women left on their own with children to care for and inadequate financial support the only option available is to rely upon parents and welfare. This could include moving back home with your parents and your children. The stress on both the children and grandparents is substantial and can be damaging to long-term family relationships. It may also impact upon your parents' income and erode part of their retirement savings. You must remember that the majority of your and your parents' retirement income will be used in your last few years of life, when you will have increased medical costs.

> *When you educate a man you educate an individual; when you educate a woman you educate a whole family.*
> – CHARLES D. MCIVER (1860–1906)

Assets

Women who are faced with divorce or the death of their partner will often hold the majority of their wealth in their homes. This is generally attributed to women being more risk averse than their male counterparts. Another reason is that women are not familiar with financial planning and other investments. They are therefore asset-rich and cash-poor. In comparison, men who are divorced or widowed are more open to the understanding of financial risk and have diversified investment portfolios. This ensures they do not have all of their capital locked away in non-productive assets. Some men also have the added benefit of a retirement fund and this is due to their employment opportunities and greater time in the workforce compared with women.

You may have heard the saying 'Behind every great man is a women'. Well, you need to start telling yourself that behind every great woman is herself, because no one but you has the drive to ensure you meet your life objectives.

Investment Clubs

Investment clubs have become popular with women in recent times. For membership to one of these clubs you will need to be assessed by the current members. Once you have been accepted you are required to pay a joining fee and adhere to the rules and conditions of your particular club. An investment club operates by its members investing a designated sum of money each month, usually under $100. This money is then invested into various stocks. Each club has an investment strategy including a realistic time frame, which is decided by the club membership so each participant understands the club goals. Individual members are expected to research investments and make recommendations to the club membership. Members then assess the information so decisions can be made on which investments to buy or sell.

Members are expected to track stocks individually and to read market and annual reports. They also learn to assess the performance growth of a good company and how other market influences can affect their particular stock. Once a club has bought its shares any profits or dividends are reinvested back into the club so that investments compound and grow.

One of the benefits of joining an investment club is you develop an understanding of how stocks and shares are bought and sold. These clubs also educate participants on how to talk with a financial professional using the right jargon. This also helps you understand what investment strategies are being suggested to you by your financial professional and why. Your experience in the investment club should assist with analysing why certain investment strategies have been suggested for your financial plan.

Some points to remember when you join an investment club:

- Risk level of each participant. Ensure the group you have joined aligns with the level of risk you're comfortable with.

- Ensure you understand the tax implications of investing and the added cost of transactions.
- Ensure there's a diversified portfolio, which spreads risk by investing in a number of industry sectors.
- Be sure that your monthly investment is money you can afford to lose.
- Understand that an investment club is a business partnership and you may be held liable for the actions of others within the club.
- Ensure you are comfortable with the procedures and processes the club has in place. You need to be sure there is a checking process for each transaction to protect against theft.
- Make sure you feel comfortable with the people in the club and that you know something about their backgrounds.

Investment clubs offer participants a great opportunity to meet and learn from a broad spectrum of the community. However, you should never rely on an investment club as your sole strategy for financial planning. As you will have learned from this book there are many factors which must be taken into account to develop a holistic approach to financial planning. Always remember each participant in your investment club has different levels of wealth, income and tax liabilities. If you are using your club as your sole investment strategy you may inadvertently create taxation or other financial hardships for yourself. The main point to remember when using investment clubs is that they are designed to educate participants on how to research and interact with the financial community. Undoubtedly the greatest benefit of an investment club is the opportunity to meet interesting people and to learn new ideas from your interaction. Always remember to consult a professional financial adviser who is qualified to provide financial advice.

Married/De Facto Women

If you are married or in a de facto relationship it is important that you create a financial plan where you budget as a unit. You both need to set realistic goals and actively work towards them. Whether you are both working or not, ensure you each have superannuation retirement plans for your future. If one partner spends more than the other and this is affecting the attainment of goals, reach an agreement to ensure future financial plans are met. It is important that each partner has some discretionary income to spend as desired without any reprisals by the other partner. Always write down all financial goals so there is never a misunderstanding of future plans and targets. (See Chapter 3, Budgeting and Chapter 4, Debt Wisdom.) Ensure you both have wills and that you are each covered by life and income protection insurance in case of any unforeseen accidents. If you have debts and/or mortgage and something happens to one partner the other may face severe financial hardship without appropriate income protection or retirement savings plans. Ensure you have seen a qualified financial adviser to assist you with your plan.

Single Mothers

Being a single mother entails many responsibilities, including an understanding of successful financial management. With so much demand on cash flow and little left to invest it is essential that no money be wasted on unnecessary purchases. If at all possible, a single mother should aim to invest some money each month. It does not matter how small the sum, a regular savings pattern will be of great benefit in times of need. Whether you own your own home, have a mortgage or rent depends greatly on your individual circumstances. If you have a financial strategy which includes the purchase of your own home, ensure you have calculated all costs associated with your purchase. Owning a home can for some put enormous pressure on the family budget and reduce the quality of life to an uncomfortable level. If you are purchasing your own home and your monthly budget is stretched to the limit you should consider renting the property out and moving into cheaper rented accommodation. If you are living on an extremely tight budget then renting suitable accommodation is a great option as you will not have any of the unplanned expenditures often associated with home ownership. By renting you will also be able to create a budget that remains constant.

If you receive any form of child support payments it is advisable that you do not rely on this money as your sole income. You should if possible gain some employment and use the child-support payment to supplement your income. If your job skills offer you very low employment prospects, do some research and use your time out of the workforce (or study part-time while working) to get some further training and then move into a better paying job. Child support payments should never be squandered and should be used on your child's education, for example on tuition, extracurricular activities or the purchase of a computer. Your financial future will suffer if you live from this income and wait until it ceases before you work out how you will support yourself. With an ageing population and reduced workforce to pay income taxes, many government pensions will be reduced to cope with escalating health costs. If you are reliant upon a government benefit you will be forced to live within a budget that you cannot control. It is always advisable to generate your own income and save for a future retirement where you know exactly what money you will receive each month.

> *Mother always said that honesty was the best policy, and money isn't everything. She was wrong about other things too.*
>
> – GERALD BARZAN

The most important issues are to ensure:

- You have a will, income protection and disability insurance to protect you and your children in case of an unforeseen medical condition or life-threatening illness.
- If you have debts including a mortgage, it is essential you have life insurance, otherwise your debtors can claim your estate to pay for your debts. This could be detrimental to your children if you don't.
- You and your children's father have a plan in place for the care of your children in case of a life-threatening illness or death.
- You live within a planned budget.
- You are planning/have a retirement fund for yourself. If you work, whether part-time, casually or full-time, a small amount of money each pay period

towards your retirement income will not be noticed if deducted automatically from your pay cheque. (Always ensure you see a reputable financial planner so your retirement income is invested into an appropriate portfolio.)

Single Women

With many opportunities now available to women, many are electing not to marry or to assume the traditional role of motherhood, opting instead for higher education and establishing a career. There is evidence which suggests the more education a woman has the less inclined she is to have many or any children. Many women are living lifestyles which include higher disposable incomes and the freedom to make their own life choices. Financial planning for these women means they need to consider how to best use their income to ensure they plan for a safe and secure financial future. It is wise to consider the following:

- Buy a home to live in that suits your current needs. (Remember location is the most important factor when purchasing a home, as it is not just a place to live but also a valuable asset that should grow in value. You should also ensure you set a specific limit on what you can afford and don't be left with a mortgage that consumes the majority of your income. Always buy in an area that is already a good area, don't risk buying in an area that may be the 'next boom area'.)
- Understand your risk tolerance level when it comes to investing.
- Ensure you have a retirement plan.
- Organise a will, and life, death and disability insurance.

Beauty

Women around the world are spending billions of dollars every year on cosmetics, hair-care, beauty treatments and plastic surgery. For some the ultimate in cosmetic alteration is to replicate their favourite celebrity's body parts; others have major plastic surgery as early as their teens. These women may not be considering the health and financial risks. What appears to be a simple medical procedure for some can in future years lead to serious health issues. As with any investment, beauty enhancements must also be assessed for the 'return on investment'. If you are contemplating major cosmetic surgery or you spend unlimited amounts of money on cosmetics, you may want to re-evaluate how this expenditure will impact upon your future. If you don't have a retirement investment plan, a plan to own your own home or other investment strategies in place you may want to reassess your current spending patterns.

To assess your beauty budget try this simple exercise. Go through your bathroom and purse and roughly calculate the cost of each item you own, including hair care products, brushes, hair accessories, make-up, face masks and other beauty treatments. Have you duplicated your purchases and bought several of the same items? You may be surprised at the amount of money you are spending on these items. Now calculate the cost of any other beauty treatments you have on a regular basis. The purpose of this exercise is to act as a wake-up call to ensure you have set realistic targets for your beauty budget. Always assess the risk of any medical procedure and ensure you have researched the complications that could arise from any cosmetic surgery. Only you can judge whether your beauty expenditure is going to have a major impact on your personal and financial lifestyle in years to come.

Heather

Heather, a mother of two, worked full-time in a business she owned with her husband at a seaside location. In her early forties she decided to have breast implants. Heather believed this would boost her self-esteem and make her feel better about herself. After the operation she felt great and did not regret having the operation. Eight years later, Heather's health deteriorated and she was diagnosed with an arthritic condition. She could no longer wear shoes without extreme discomfort. Her hands swelled and her back became stiff. Her quality of life fell to the point where she could no longer function independently. Her greatest regret was the energy she had wasted on plastic surgery, energy she desperately needed now to fight the pain of her illness.

Health

> *Your prayers should be for a healthy mind in a healthy body.*
> – JUVENAL (C. 60–130)

Women often live longer than men. As we age, cancer and other illnesses are more common, so we need to ensure we have access to funds to pay for our increasing health costs. In particular women often face extended living expenses and the possibility of dependent health care. Studies indicate that women will visit a medical practitioner more readily than a man, and this contributes to escalating health costs. As new medical technology is developed the standard of health care is constantly improving, and this translates to greater access to modern medical equipment with added costs.

There are many health issues women may avoid later in life if they take the time and effort to practise a healthy lifestyle throughout their life. Developing a conscious awareness of healthy living will also ensure your finances will last as long as you do. Some health issues for women to consider are:

- Osteoporosis – Brittle bones caused by the diet not containing enough calcium. Also caused by lack of weight-bearing exercise.
- Diet-induced diabetes – a condition caused by poor diet containing too much fat and/or sugar. In the 21st century this is going to be one of the major contributors which will increase the cost of health care nation-wide.

- Obesity – caused by eating more food than your body burns up in kilojoules. Often it is due to consuming too much fat and sugar in too many takeaway meals, or just poor eating habits. This disease will also contribute to escalating health costs to individuals via rises in private health insurance premiums and in governments' health budgets.
- Smoking – Younger women are smoking more than men, often with the aim of staying slim. If a smoker's exercise and diet are not adequate, osteoporosis, hardening arteries, emphysema and other illnesses are more likely to contribute to poor health. These illnesses also contribute to escalating health costs.

> *To lengthen thy life, lessen thy meals.*
> — BENJAMIN FRANKLIN (1706–1790)

These are just a few of the diseases which will affect our ageing population. For those of us who never exercise, eat balanced meals, **detoxify** or spend time in nature, our old age may entail discomfort and financial stress. Spending time on your own, whether it be walking, dancing or just moving, is not just important to your physical wellbeing but it also contributes to your emotional health. It is never too late to re-evaluate your current lifestyle, eliminate unhealthy habits and adopt healthier alternatives.

> *Everyone dreams: but not equally. Those who dream by night in the dusty recesses of their minds wake in the day to find that it was vanity; but the dreamers of the day are dangerous people, for they may act their dream with open eyes, to make it possible.*
> — T. E. LAWRENCE (1888–1935)

Summary

- For some women extreme debt and poverty is a major threat to their financial security.
- Many women ignore or neglect to examine the way in which they live and spend.
- Women need to develop financial self-sufficiency, whether they are married, in a de facto relationship or single.
- Regardless of marital status, all women should have a full understanding of their finances, and a will, life and death insurance, and retirement savings plan.
- Women need to start a savings plan early to ensure a comfortable retirement.
- Women spend more time out of the workforce than men and this can be attributed to having children, caring for an ill relative or they may return to school to upgrade their skills.
- Any advantage you can give yourself to make yourself financially secure is worth the effort.
- Don't waste your life waiting for a knight in shining armour to save you from your financial problems.
- There are many health issues women may avoid later in life if they take the time and effort to practise a healthy lifestyle throughout their life.

10

Retirement Planning

[Of leaner times in his life]
There were times my pants were so thin I could sit
on a dime and tell if it was heads or tails
— SPENCER TRACY (1900–67)

> *To be poor and independent is very nearly an impossibility.*
> – WILLIAM COBBETT (1762–1835)

Planning for your retirement is something all people in modern society have to do. As our society's ageing population increases, it is probable that governments will be unable to offer the same level of assistance received by retired people today. In the future many elderly citizens will face the prospect of living below the poverty line, and not being able to access government support. This is a common global phenomenon throughout the developed world.

There is a growing proportion of people aged between 40 and 55 years of age, commonly identified as the baby boomer generation. As these people retire from work over the next thirty years, their places in the workforce will not be fully replaced by the next generation. Most countries are attempting to deal with this problem by increasing or abolishing compulsory retirement ages. However, a recent survey clearly illustrates that most people are planning to retire before they reach 60 years of age, and not the 70 years of age that the country's political leaders would prefer. Research also indicates baby boomers are often unaware of the inadequacy of their retirement plans. A common view among this generation is that if you own your home, your retirement is secured. However, selling the family home does not form part of the retirement strategy. No planning is given as to where or how income can be derived from a house to provide a retirement income stream. Typically, baby boomers massively underestimate the amount required to fund their retirement at an adequate level. One of the common explanations is that they are likely to inherit substantial wealth from their parents. In reality, however, their parents are still living and using their wealth. The fastest growing group in our population is the over 80s. If these parents become ill, then their money will be needed to fund their medical expenses. A recent study found that most people spent more than 50 per cent of their whole life's medical expenses in the final year of their life.

In general the younger generations are not adequately planning for their retirement either. There is a continual focus on the accumulation of lifestyle assets such as cars, motorcycles, sound systems and TVs, before wealth accumulation and retirement planning. The earlier people plan for retirement, the easier it is to accumulate the appropriate amount of investment assets. In some countries retirement funds are not accessible until a designated retirement age. While it is reasonable for young people not to want to tie up funds for 25 or 30 years, they will benefit from focusing on acquiring a home or other capital assets (investment or business) as early as possible. Ideally you should open retirement accounts and place the minimum permissible contributions into those accounts from the day you start full-time work. If your employer contributes on your behalf and you are not required to contribute, then don't. Focus on home ownership or other investment options.

What are Your Retirement Goals?

Let's examine what is required in retirement. First, you need to determine exactly what your goals are, and what income is needed in retirement. The best place to start is by re-examining the budget that you completed in Chapter 3. Secondly, you need to consider those expenses you won't have in retirement, such as mortgage expenses (your house will be paid off by then!), retirement savings and business expenses (such as business clothing, and second motor vehicles). These expenses can be removed from your budget, but you do need to add back any expected increases such as more holiday expenditure, sporting club memberships, and green fees for all you golfers (!). Most people believe they will spend less in retirement, but when retired find they actually need to scale back their lifestyle in order to live within their available means.

This exercise will enable you to set more realistic financial goals for your retirement. Remember, it is also likely your medical expenses will gradually increase as you age. Also remember to adjust this expense amount for inflation.

Funding Your Retirement

It is likely that if you are 20 years from retirement you will not be eligible to receive a government pension, due to the increased costs caused by an ageing population. If you are part of a company pension plan, you should ask the fund administrator for an estimate of your likely retirement benefit.

If you know what your existing retirement savings are likely to provide, you then need to ensure that you can accumulate the 'gap' amount between what you've got and what you need. When you are estimating growth rates for investments, it is better to use a conservative earnings rate even for growth investments (say 8–10 per cent for equities, less for property, cash, and fixed interest).

Other countries have similar tax advantaged schemes, such as superannuation (retirement fund) in Australia, which permit tax deductible contributions and have a low tax rate on investment earnings and growth. The superannuation system is complicated and most people will need the assistance of a professional adviser during changes of employment, and for retirement planning. Retirement planning strategies can add hundreds of thousands of dollars to investors' investment portfolios, so always consult a professional financial adviser.

A mistake many young people make in managing their retirement monies is to invest too conservatively. If you are more than twenty years from retirement, you should be investing in growth assets only, that is, domestic and international shares and property. Some investment advisers are far too cautious when it comes to assessing an appropriate asset allocation for the very long term.

The types of risk profiles appropriate for other investors is dependent upon the usual factors including long term and risk tolerance. Your financial adviser can assist you in ensuring that your asset allocation is appropriate for your individual circumstances.

The other end of funding your retirement is the drawing of income streams or capital amounts for funding your daily living expenses. In some countries, individuals have almost an obsession with the idea that you should never sell a capital asset for the purpose of spending the funds on living expenses. As a financial adviser Jonathan has never been able to understand this attitude: money is essentially a commodity to be utilised in the most appropriate way at any time. Whether funds are investment capital or income is of no consequence to the money, so why should it determine the behaviour of the owner.

You also need to ensure that your retirement income stream is drawn from the most tax effective environment possible. For example, in Australia many retirees withdraw their accumulated retirement accounts as lump sums, ignoring a range of tax incentives to encourage people to utilise retirement income streams. Again, your financial adviser can assist in ensuring that you pursue an appropriate strategy.

It is a worthy goal to accumulate sufficient funds during your working life to maintain a reasonable standard of living in retirement, however, be prepared to spend the lot over your retirement. Many people don't realise they will need all of their accumulated funds to maintain their current standard of living. They often believe they will be able to live and leave large sums of money to their children. Most parents need their money to live on and have decent medical care. In other words, assume you will spend all the funds you have accumulated over your lifetime. It used to be quite common for clients to anticipate declining demand for retirement income especially once they passed 75 years. However, with the costs of medical care, it is Jonathan's view that these assumptions are not appropriate and you should expect that your cost of living will not decrease but rather its use will change with your health and accommodation needs. (See Chapter 11, Baby Boomers' Financial Awakening for the Retirement Budget.)

Summary

- Many people are inadequately funded for a comfortable retirement.
- The earlier you plan for retirement, the easier it is to accumulate the appropriate amount of investment assets.
- Most people believe they will spend less in retirement, but when retired find they actually need to scale back their lifestyle in order to live within their available means.
- The type of risk profiles appropriate for retirees' investments is dependent on the usual factors including the time horizon and risk tolerance.

11

The Baby Boomers' Financial Awakening

*It is **strange** that the one thing that every person looks forward to, namely old age, is the one thing for which no preparation is made.*

— John Dewey (1859–1952)

Many baby boomers have started re-inventing retirement and are ensuring that age is no restriction when it comes to enjoying life and new experiences. This group, born between 1946 and 1964, is committed to avoiding the traditional way their parents and other retirees lived and were seen by younger generations. This includes farewelling the signs of premature ageing, such as grey hair, comfortable shoes and physical unfitness. This new generation invented consumerism, fought for equality for women and revolutionised sexual freedom with the introduction of the pill. Is it any wonder they are still pushing the boundaries when today's issues, such as divorce, remarriage, menopause (male and female), sexual impotence and retirement planning are openly discussed and debated. This group is not afraid to live for the moment, and are determined to seize and enjoy every day.

> *You can't be old without money.*
> — CAT ON A HOT TIN ROOF, TENNESSEE WILLIAMS (1911–83)

Realistically, although the baby boomer generation may have a zest for a youthful retirement lifestyle, they need to make sacrifices in order to save the necessary income to fund their retirement. Previous retirees did not expect to live more than 10 years in retirement, having worked to 65 years. Baby boomers enjoy increasing access to advanced medical care and healthier food and lifestyles, thereby living 20 to 30 years in retirement. This is a daunting thought: funding the retirement lifestyle you desire, you may need to make significant financial changes to your current spending patterns to reach your goal.

At the beginning of the twentieth century the average age for retirement was 65 and the average person was expected to live one to five years in retirement. Usually their employer paid employees a retirement wage or the government paid a pension that assisted people during retirement. Today it is becoming increasingly unlikely that we will be able to rely on government pensions to fund even part of our retirement. With a growing proportion of aged people in our population, a reduction in birth rates and a reduced workforce in western countries, the income governments derive from taxation, especially income tax, will be significantly reduced in the future. Ageing populations increase the demands on government health care budgets and place added pressure on government pensions. The reduction in funds from income tax will also affect government services that we expect to be available as we grow old.

Caring for Elderly Parents

For some baby boomers there is an expectation they will be able to generate part of their retirement income from inherited money. This may be a feasible option, but it should be noted that the cost of aged health care and dependency care is on the increase. The over-65 age group today will use most of their income to pay for health and medical costs. Many older people will need to be cared for in facilities that offer 24-hour medical care. In Australia a facility with 24-hour care can cost as much as $60,000 per year.

Charles and Paul

Charles is a 75-year-old widower. Two years ago he had to move into a 24-hour aged care facility after he fell and broke his hip. Leaving his home of 30 years was very difficult for Charles but he knew he couldn't cope on his own. His only son, Paul, a doctor, had recently divorced, which meant he had to divide his assets and savings with his former spouse and money was limited. Charles had some funds from the sale of his home in a savings account and a small portfolio of shares he had to sell. This was the only income he had available to fund his living costs. Next year Charles will only have limited savings left to live from, so his son has three options. The first is to move his father from his current residential care facility to a more economical one, which will offer his father limited health care. Second, he could move his father into his own home, which seems inappropriate due to his father's need for 24-hour care; or third, he could fund the cost of his father's 24-hour care himself. Charles did not want to leave his current residential care facility so he and Paul decided the best option was for Paul to pay for his father's care.

For many elderly people today, their first choice is to stay in their own

> *Change is not made without inconvenience, even from worse to better.*
> – RICHARD HOOKER (1554–1600)

home as long as possible. For some this option will not be possible due to the increasing cost of private nursing care, the cost of hiring a live-in companion and/or the added cost of home maintenance services. Some baby boomers may find the services offered by public health facilities inadequate and the escalating cost of private health insurance inappropriate for their parents' care. The only option left for some is to find suitable residential care for their parents and assist them with the costs after any government subsidies have been deducted. These added costs may affect the choice of lifestyle you will be able to fund for your retirement.

As with all things in life, nothing is ever certain. You may never have to consider for your parents any of the health care issues raised here, but it is always wise to prepare for the unforeseen.

Reality Check

> *If I'd known I was going to live this long, I'd have taken better care of myself.*
> – EUBIE BLAKE (1883–1983), WHO DIED FIVE DAYS AFTER HIS HUNDREDTH BIRTHDAY

For baby boomers there is a financial awakening in facing the reality that the time to save and adequately prepare for your retirement is running out. You may think that retirement is something you don't need to consider yet. You may have more pressing issues to think about, such as paying off your home, renovating the kitchen or planning your next holiday. Never forget that financial lifestyle planning is a holistic approach to living. While you may believe your employment situation will remain ongoing and your quality of life will be maintained you can never be sure this is the case. Many people are made redundant or lose their jobs in their 40s and 50s when they need to prepare for retirement. Some people are forced into early retirement in their early 50s and may never be able to find another job that will meet their financial needs.

- If you were forced into early retirement or made redundant tomorrow how would you be affected financially?
- Could you pay off your credit cards or other debts?
- Do you know how much income your retirement pension would pay you weekly?

It is always wise to save for a rainy day and not to live beyond your means. The reality is nothing in life is certain. Remember 11 September 2001 and the impact this unimaginable tragedy had, not just on Americans, but also on many people from different countries, as it affected employment, financial security and global security. Employees of major airlines and many people in the tourism sector lost their jobs overnight.

The reality for many baby boomers is they are not actively planning their retirement. Traditional retirement ages are no longer enforced, which means many workers expecting to retire at age 55 to 60 may not be able to afford to do so until they are 70 or older. As well as the cost burden of an ageing population we also have an increase in life expectancy. A baby born in 2002 has a projected life expectancy of 104. A man of 50 in 2002 has a life expectancy of over 80, and a woman of

> *Be happy while you're living, for you're a long time dead.*
> – ANONYMOUS (SCOTTISH MOTTO)

> *Always remember life is not a dress rehearsal, it is reality.*
> – ANONYMOUS

50 has a life expectancy of 85 or more. If you retire at 55 you can expect to live to 80–85 or more, and you will need 30 years of income to live from. For many this is longer than we may have actually worked. It also means we may have to find some part-time employment during our retirement years to ensure we have enough income to live. This whole shift will place an added tax burden on the younger generations to support retirees. We have to expect that there may well be a backlash against unfair and unsustainable tax burdens. This is an issue governments need to act upon now.

In the UK, the USA and some parts of Europe, government taxes fund part of retirement pensions. This is seen as a way to pay back citizens for all the years of taxation they paid to the government. This style of pension may prove to be unsustainable. In Australia, the government made it law in 1986 that all full-time workers be part of the retirement funding scheme of superannuation. The government legislated for a compulsory contribution from employers towards employees' retirement savings. That contribution is now 9 per cent of an Australian's income. For Australians, saving for your own retirement fund is not unusual. However, many are inadequately funded and government may be called upon to assist those who find their incomes insufficient. No matter what age you are now, retirement will be an issue one day and you need to educate yourself on how you can best prepare for it.

Planning for Retirement

The reality for most baby boomers is they are not focusing on retirement issues. Too many believe they are adequately funded for retirement because they already contribute towards a retirement fund and they plan to own their home when they do retire. Owning your own home is only part of the equation for retirement. A home is a sleeping asset unless you plan to sell it and use the funds to generate more income for yourself or borrow against the equity and negatively gear into shares or other investments.

Other issues to consider include the age you must be before you can access your superannuation monies. If you are made redundant, lose your job or are forced to retire due to poor health you will need access to income to fund your living expenses until your reach retirement age. Examine your current portfolio and ensure you have investments which can be easily liquidated. If your current portfolio consists of your home and your superannuation monies and nothing else, you need to seek some financial advice on how to increase your asset holdings without placing too much pressure on your current lifestyle. Even if you never face the prospect of losing your job or becoming ill, the added investments will increase the quality of your life when you eventually retire.

While many baby boomers enjoy a high standard of living, many are not consciously considering the cost of their current lifestyles. Spending vast sums of money on dead assets will be paid for in retirement. Needing to draw on the equity in your home to purchase cars, go on a holiday, renovate or pay off excessive credit card bills is a warning that you are living beyond your means. Having your bank revalue your home so you can increase your borrowing limit should only be undertaken for investment purposes.

Using the equity in your home to purchase unprofitable assets (a new sofa, TV, entertainment unit, cars, etc.) which are not diversified investments is not wise as these assets don't generate any income, and can't be sold quickly. Some people claim their home is an investment and they justify drawing on the equity in the home to renovate as acceptable, but in reality a home is a sleeping asset until you sell it. It doesn't generate any income while you live in it (unless you negatively gear into alternative investments such as shares or another property). You can't just sell off a bathroom to recoup some of your money if you need it in a hurry. You must sell off the whole house to recoup the investment.

The real point is if you are going to use the equity in your home, it should be used for investments that form part of a diversified portfolio and deliver passive investment income. Using the excuse that interest rates on your home are cheaper than your credit card provider or other money providers is also not an excuse to start eating into your home equity. Your goal should always be to pay your home off as fast as you can and then use the equity to fund other income generating investments.

As with any investment strategy it is important you understand the risks associated with your investment choice, and the time frame for your investment as it is part of an overall plan to help you reach your goal. Be aware that statistically the likelihood is that baby boomers will generate most of their wealth in their 40s and 50s. If you start eroding your assets (such as your home) you will never pay them off or you will end up using some of your retirement lump sum to pay off the debt you have incurred.

Remember, any money or assets you own should only be used to generate a passive income. Before you cash in any worthwhile asset such as your home or other investments, always consider how this will impact on your retirement and whether it will erode your overall wealth. Everything you buy today has to be paid for – if not today, then tomorrow. Take care to understand what you are doing, thereby ensuring any investment choice generates income.

When implementing any new investment strategy there are many factors which must be accounted for, including:

- How many years is it until you plan to retire?
- How much debt do you currently service?
- How much income is generated from your investments?
- What investment goals do you need to meet on the day you retire?
- How much money is currently in your retirement fund?
- How much income will you need to live on in retirement?
- What government benefits will be available when you do retire?
- What taxes will you have to pay on your retirement lump sum?
- How long will it take you to pay off your home (if you currently have a mortgage)?
- How long will it take to buy a home if you don't?
- How long will it take for you to pay off all of your current debt?
- What emergency funds can you cash in if you become ill in retirement and cannot care for yourself?
- Would you be able to retire comfortably if you lost your job tomorrow, in two years' time, or in five?
- Do you have a budget?

Retirement planning should not be disregarded until you reach your few final years of full-time employment. It is an issue you should assess and budget for from the day you start employment. The longer you procrastinate about your retirement plan the harder it will be to save.

We have included two charts for you to fill out detailing your current home loan debt, along with some illustrative examples.

- You need to detail any loans you have used against the equity in your home and what you used the money for.
- Make sure you clarify if the investment choices you made generate income or whether the funds were used to purchase dead assets. Your choices may have deferred your retirement date and/or altered the lifestyle you will be able to fund during your retirement.
- You must also assess how much interest has contributed to your overall debt.
- How long it will take to pay off your debts.

> *If a man will begin with certainties, he shall end in doubts; but if he will be content to begin with doubts, he shall end in certainties.*
>
> — FRANCIS BACON (1561–1626)

Once again, be honest when filling in these charts otherwise you won't get a complete picture of your current asset worth.

Current Home Loan Chart

Value of home loan	$400,000 (example)
Length of home loan	30 years
Interest	8%
Current monthly repayments	$2935
Principal repaid	$400,000
Interest paid	$658,686
Total	$1,058,686

The graph on page 172 shows how a standard home loan is repaid over time.

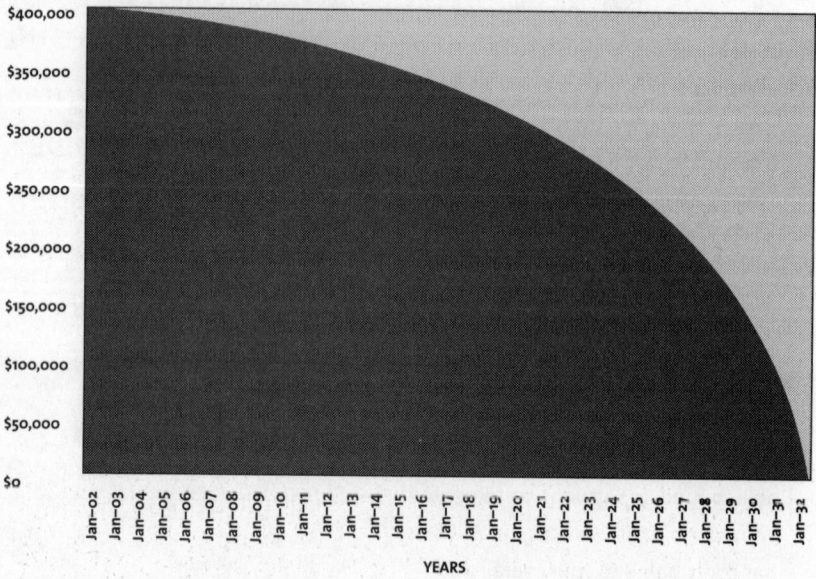

Borrowing on Equity in Home Loan

The next chart details what happens to your home loan debt if you use the equity in your home to purchase consumer items such as cars and holidays. You must always remember to note whether the money borrowed is going to generate an income or whether it is for a dead asset such as consumer spending. In this example we have assumed that the latter is the case.

Original loan	$400,000
Equity in home in year 16	$200,000
Amount borrowed against equity	$150,000
Interest	8%
Years to pay off new loan	15
Monthly repayments	$2935 + $1433
Income generated from new borrowings	Nil
Principal repaid	$550,000
Interest paid	$768,632
Total	**$1,318,632**

The graph below shows that the repayment of the debt within the original term of the loan requires an increase in repayments to $4368 per month.

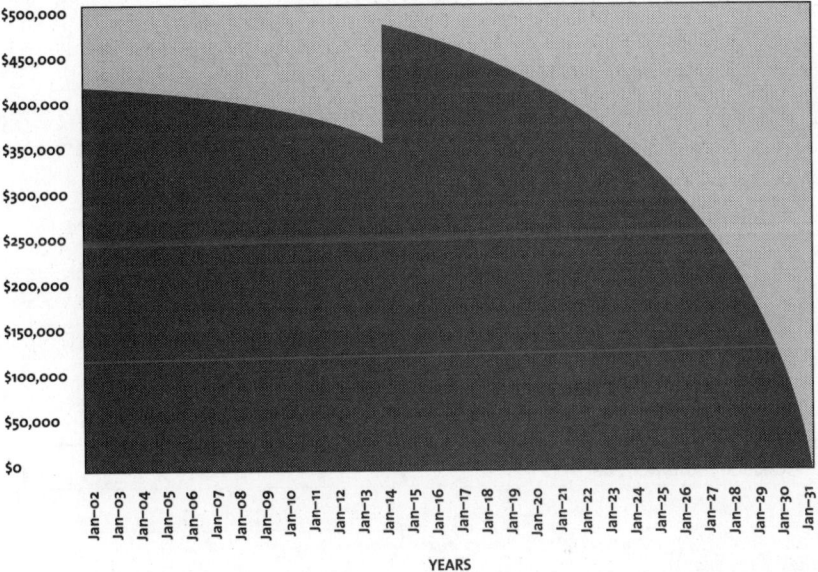

If you simply maintained the original repayment schedule then the additional loan would take 10 extra years to repay.

If you put the money spent on interest for the extra funds as an additional repayment off the original loan then the term of the loan would be reduced by seven years. There are a number of options open to home owners when reviewing their position in respect to their mortgage, and we suggest that you seek some professional advice from your accountant or financial adviser before purchasing a new car, boat, renovation or other consumer item.

Designing Your Retirement Plan

Developing realistic goals is one of the hardest aspects when designing your retirement. We all have expectations of what retirement will be, yet we neglect to actively examine all the costs associated with our choices.

Many of us may fail to examine the impact our current spending patterns will have on our retirement lifestyle.

Preselect a retirement date so that you have a set time frame to work within. In the chart below list everything you envisage for your retirement.

- At this stage don't include any costs.
- Don't be afraid to list everything you may wish for, as no one but you ever has to see this chart.
- If you are married or in a relationship get your partner to fill out their retirement goals on a separate sheet of paper so you can compare your thoughts.
- Don't forget to include all your leisure activities or hobbies.

Designing Retirement Goals Chart

Proposed retirement date

Examine your completed Designing Retirement Goals Chart. With this information you know what you are working towards.

- Now on your Proposed Retirement Plan chart (see below), cost out all of the *items* you listed on the first chart and items you plan to acquire before you retire.

- Exclude any leisure activities from the second chart. List only the items you will be purchasing for your retirement. If this includes, for example, golf buggy or golf clubs, include such items.
- Will you be moving from your current home? Going interstate? Purchasing new furniture, cars, boats etc?

This important process will assist you to establish a savings plan ensuring you meet these goals before you retire.

You must be totally honest with yourself and realistic about the cost needed to reach these targets.

You will also need to add inflation as items cost more with time.

Proposed Retirement Plan

Item	Funds Available	Funds Needed	Funds to be Borrowed or Saved	Time Frame (Years to retirement)	Annual Cost to be Saved
House	$200,000	$150,000	$150,000	12 years	$2,500
Car	$30,000	$30,000			
Golf Buggy	$15,000				

Note: the costs of desired assets may be funded by the sale of other assets, for example the second car.

Weekly Expenditure

The next process requires you to detail what you envisage a typical week in retirement will be: what you will do, what you will buy, entertainment, sport etc.

Note: Often you do more than one activity on a particular day, so you need to ensure you expand the chart to include all daily activities and their cost. A chart needs to be completed for all members of the household who will be using the retirement budget.

Day	Activity	Cost	Meals in/out	Estimated Cost	Total
Monday					
Morning	Play golf	$60.00			
Afternoon			Out	$25.00	(example)
Evening	Dinner x 2		Out	$100.00	
(Example)	Concert	$90.00			$355.00
Tuesday					
Morning					
Afternoon					
Evening					
Wednesday					
Morning					
Afternoon					
Evening					
Thursday					
Morning					
Afternoon					
Evening					
Friday					
Morning					
Afternoon					
Evening					
Saturday					
Morning					
Afternoon					
Evening					
Sunday					
Morning					
Afternoon					
Evening					
Total					

Services

Identify what services you will need in retirement or that you currently use, that you will add to or may drop from your budget. (Think about the services your parents needed or used in retirement as a guide to assist you.)

Service	Times used per week/month	Cost	Plan to use/in use	Weekly Total	Annual Total
House cleaned (example)	2 days a week	$60 x 2	both	$120.00	$6,240.00
Gardener					
House cleaned					
Laundry-ironing					
Pool cleaner					
Manicure					
Pedicure					
Massage					
Facial					
Hairdresser					
Groceries delivered					
Visit Doctor/Dentist/Analyst					
Personal trainer					
Pet washed/groomed					
Carer					
Transport other than car					
Other					
Total					

Items Bought/Sold

Decide what you will buy and sell for the first stage of your retirement.

Item	Buy/Sell	Sold For	New Cost	Need to Borrow	Total
House (example)	Both (upgrading)	$300,000	$490,000	$190,000	$190,000 Negative
Car own 2 – sell one (example)	sell	$15,000	na	na	$15,000 Positive

Estimated Retirement Living Costs

Calculate the age you must work to and estimate the income you believe you need for living costs in retirement. (Do not take into consideration the tax payable on this lump sum.) You must remember these are not the only funds you will need if you are considering moving house or buying a new car or going on a holiday etc.

Item	Age Now	Retirement Age	Years to Retirement	Estimated Annual Income	Lump Sum Needed
Example	43	55	12	$40,000	$480,000
You					
Partner					

Debts

Assess your current debt and liabilities and the length of time you will need to pay for these. Include: credit card debt, house, car, personal loans, child support payments, business debts, etc.

Balance Item	Timeframe of Debt	Interest of Debt	Total Rate	Cost
House (example)	$100,000	10 years	7.5%	$145,685
Credit card (example)	$9,000	10 years	16%	$18,621
Personal loan (example)	$25,000	10 years	9.8%	$40,337

Eliminating Unnecessary Spending

You're now in the position to see where your money is going and how much impact unnecessary spending could have on your retirement. Review your expenditure and decide which services and other costs you want to eliminate to reach your income goal for retirement.

Item	Weekly/ Monthly Cost to be Deleted from Budget	Annual Total Saved	Years to Retirement	Value to Retirement Fund (at 8%)
House cleaned (example)	$120.00 weekly	$6,240 Reinvested	12	$125,064

The main purpose for these charts is to ensure you understand the real cost of your retirement. You may have envisaged an ideal retirement and have only a vague idea of how you propose to fund retirement. If you wish to achieve your ideal you must plan it in detail and write down what you realistically can afford. With the charts complete you will understand why it is imperative you start planning immediately. With this realisation you need to set your financial goals throughout your working career to reach your target. Without a plan for your retirement you may struggle to achieve the retirement lifestyle you desire.

The work sheets above should enable you to determine your capital and income requirements in retirement. In the next section you will be asked to transfer the numbers you have just come up with into the Baby Boomer Budget Chart which will help you set your saving and investing priorities between now and retirement.

These charts reinforce the idea that life is all about choice. If you don't plan for the future, you definitely won't have enough time to save for your desired retirement income. You may now realise your expectations for your retirement are beyond your means and you need to re-examine your choices, such as:

- your estimate of weekly spending in retirement
- the size and location of your proposed retirement home
- the number of motor vehicles, boats, motorbikes etc. you plan on owning or maintaining and running
- the number of holidays per year and destination
- the amount of dining out and takeaway meals.

From the completed charts above you now know what savings you will need in retirement. Now you need to set up a budgeting system that will ensure you meet your financial goals.

Baby Boomer Budget

A budget designed for you as a baby boomer must make clear the sacrifices necessary for you to reach your goals for retirement. Should you falter from your budget you will not meet your commitments and therefore will not have the retirement lifestyle you plan. From the previous section (Designing Your Retirement Plan), you should have worked out what goals you wish to achieve for your retirement. Now you need to devise a strategy to secure these goals.

As with the Money Karma Budget, this budget is personal and specifically relates to the amount of income you need in retirement. We all live, earn and spend differently and you are the only one who can design a budget that will meet all of your emotional and financial requirements. Be honest and realistic with the lifestyle you are planning for your retirement.

Establishing this budget may be timely and may frustrate you, but it only needs to be done once and reviewed yearly or whenever you experience a change in your circumstances. This planning will inevitably make the financial transition from work to retirement easier. This budget should ensure your finances in retirement will be as near as possible to how you planned. Always consult a certified financial planner before you implement any financial strategies as he/she will be able to ensure you meet your goals without attracting any unforseen liabilities.

When completing the Baby Boomer Budget Chart ensure you account for your partner and include their retirement dates and monies as appropriate.

Baby Boomer Budget Chart

Your proposed retirement date	25 December 2012 (example)
Number of working years left until retirement	10 years
Current amount in your superannuation	$150,000
Amount contributed per year for retirement	$15,000
Estimated superannuation lump sum on retirement	$541,000
Your proposed annual retirement income	$40,000
Total amount of debt to be cleared before you retire	House: $200,000 Credit cards, car, other loans: $75,000
Funds left after debt is repaid	$266,000
The gap needed (if any) between your estimated retirement lump sum and your proposed annual retirement income	$184,000
Retirement house fund (if you are planning to move or upgrade your house when you retire). List the extra money you will need to save for upgrade	Moving interstate,. new house need extra $100,000
Retirement leisure gear to purchase (if you plan to play golf, ski, paint on a regular basis the cost of goods to buy)	Buying golf cart: $15,000 New clubs: $2000
Estimated funding shortfall	$301,000

In the above example the person can improve their position by dealing with their level of debt while they are still in the workforce. However, they will need to find three times the savings that they intended in order to make a material difference to their retirement position.

The charts in this chapter are designed to be the catalyst to help you change your financial future. You should now have an understanding of the issues you need to focus on to secure a comfortable retirement.

In life nothing is ever certain. For many baby boomers there are external factors which will complicate and alter their retirement goals. These include divorce, remarriage, the death of a partner or any other changes you may encounter. Those who may divorce or remarry will need to factor in the impact a new family will have on their retirement goals. Some who remarry may restart the journey of parenthood with step-children, or have new children with their new partner, while still supporting and caring for children from past relationships.

You must consider the impact any change will have on your retirement plans. Although this is largely dependent on your overall wealth and current lifestyle, sometimes changes mean you will need to rethink your retirement date and proposed income. We only have a limited time to generate income and save, therefore it is essential you value every cent you earn and always live within a budget.

Sally and Edward

Sally was 55, has been divorced for two years and has four children aged 22, 24, 25 and 27. She lived in a townhouse in the suburbs. Sally worked as a casual cleaner at the local hospital and never contributed to any retirement fund. Through a mutual friend she met Edward, also 55, a public servant who had two sons, aged 29 and 30. He had a compulsory retirement fund, which he contributed to for over 32 years. Shortly after they married they decided to sell her townhouse and live in Edward's house. The sale of the townhouse only generated $60,000 after the mortgage was paid out. With this money she and Edward decided to purchase a new car for $35,000 and go on an overseas holiday. The holiday cost $15,000, but the couple justified their spending by convincing each other they had worked all their lives and deserved a break.

Sally retired soon after her marriage and Edward worked for two more years before he retired. Sally and Edward both knew he was going to get a lump sum and pension on the day he retired. His pension was going to be *approximately $22,500 per annum (indexed). This was going to have to support both of them as Sally had generated no income for her retirement. She was waiting for the old age pension to help support them both. A few months before Edward retired the pair went on another two-week holiday.*

The day Edward retired Sally organised a surprise holiday to Tahiti to celebrate Edward's retirement. Sally and Edward had planned to move interstate to retire near the coast, but were shocked at the cost of housing in their desired location. They had never done any research and just assumed they could sell their current home and move. Money became an issue which they seemed to argue about all the time. As the couple owned two cars they decided to sell one and pay off some credit card debt. Edward had planned to play golf as part of his retirement hobby but no longer had the income to afford his sport regularly. Both Sally and Edward were forced to live the reality that retirement does not just happen, it must be planned.

Where to Invest When you Retire

Once you reach your desired retirement age you will be confronted with many issues, including what to do with your lump sum. Remember this money has to last for the rest of your life. You need to ensure you invest it in an environment that will make it last. For many of us this lump sum will be the largest sum of money we hold at any one time. The important point is that this will generally be the last amount of money you will receive once you stop working.

It is vital that you never view this money as a lottery win, to be spent on items you have not budgeted for. Never draw down any of this money until you have examined your options with a Certified Financial Planner (CFP) if you have not already done so. Your CFP should educate you on investment opportunities, ensuring your lump sum generates the income you need to live on, without attracting high fee charges, management costs and taxes. Your CFP should also disclose any commissions they will receive for investing your money and the percentage they bill you for the long-term management of your investment.

Once you are satisfied your CFP meets all of your ethical requirements and they have fully disclosed all of the fees and charges associated with your investment, your retirement planning costs become part of your budget expenses. As with any professional service you get what you pay for.

There are several options available for retired investors to consider. Always keep in mind you are selecting an investment vehicle which will make your money last as long as possible. This means you must be astute about the interest paid on your lump sum and the risk associated with your choice of investment.

Listed below are some investment options available for your retirement income.

Allocated Pension

This option is only available to citizens of Australia. An allocated pension is a type of retirement income stream that can only be started with superannuation (retirement) funds. This is the most common form of retirement income stream in Australia because it delivers a tax effective regular income stream, but preserves access to capital should the investor need funds. The investment risk is up to the investor, as the underlying investment in an allocated pension can be growth focused or very conservative. Most allocated pensions cost the user between 1.7 and 2.2 per cent per year. The tax payable by an allocated pension fund on income and earnings is nil, however the income stream is taxed in the hands of the investor on a concessional basis (where there is a tax free amount and a 15 per cent rebate). If you live in Australia and have money accumulated in superannuation we recommend that you seek professional advice prior to commencing any retirement income streams, otherwise you will probably pay too much income tax throughout your retirement.

Annuity

Unlike the allocated pension, an annuity is the same thing the world over. It is an agreed income stream that can be purchased from a financial business. They can be structured to suit the investor's particular needs, such as being paid without using any of the capital money invested (100 per cent residual capital), or being paid so that all of the capital is eventually paid out (nil residual value). Annuities last for the contracted term or lifetime. The benefits of annuities are that they eliminate the investment risk for the investor and deliver certainty in terms of income.

Term Deposits

Term Deposits are a fixed interest investment provided by banks, building societies and credit unions. They are amongst the most conservative of investment choices available to investors. There is little or no risk associated with this type of investment and they usually yield correspondingly low returns.

Investing Too Conservatively

Some people don't ever invest in anything other than bank deposits and term deposits. The risk associated with this selection is that the investor will not receive enough investment return to fund their retirement. Most bank-guaranteed investments barely provide investment returns above the rate of inflation, which dooms investors to after tax returns approaching nil per cent.

Tax Effective Investments

Any investment that promotes tax savings as a main feature can be termed a tax effective investment. The value of this investment should be assessed in the same manner as any other investment by looking at returns, time frame and investment risk. The tax implications should be considered in the context of normal investment criteria. A characteristic of many tax effective investments is the length of time your money is invested before you get a return. Buyer beware when selecting an investment that delivers high levels of tax efficiency as often they are promoted with a current taxation ruling that can be overturned if the promoters fail to deliver the investment specified in the offer document. A number of schemes have had their tax rulings overturned and the investors are liable to repay tax deductions.

Self-Managed Superannuation

Self-managed superannuation is when you have DIY (Do It Yourself) retirement funds. Typically these funds are favoured by asset-rich individuals or business people seeking to maximise their control over the funds investments. Investors interested in using DIY options should consult a professional accountant and financial planner who will assist with administration and regulatory issues.

Baby Boomer Retirement Checklist

1	Have you completed your Baby Boomer Budget?	Yes/No
2	Do you know what your projected retirement income will be?	Yes/No
3	Have you completed the charts within this chapter?	Yes/No
4	Have you clearly identified your retirement leisure goals?	Yes/No
5	Have you consulted a Certified Financial Planner?	Yes/No
6	Do you have a will? Is it up to date?	Yes/No
7	Are you actively improving your overall physical wellbeing?	Yes/No
8	Have you accumulated enough capital to retire?	Yes/No
9	If you have not, do you have a strategy to fund your lifestyle in retirement?	Yes/No
10	Are you aware of all the government benefits you are entitled to?	Yes/No

Managing Change

Designing your pathway for future retirement can be very difficult. The transition involves identifying new priorities and responsibilities. We spend the majority of our lives planning around the needs of our family and occupation. If you are a dentist you are defined by this label, the same applies for a doctor, lawyer, plumber, hairdresser, mother, father, gardener, teacher and so on. Once you are retired, these occupational labels are less important. You have the freedom to do whatever you choose, in your own time and for your own satisfaction. The reality is the transition from who you were at work to what you want to do in retirement is an overwhelming challenge every retiree faces.

Retirement offers opportunities to pursue new challenges and possibly new careers. Planning for your life in retirement requires as much energy, research and effort as preparing for your financial security. Many new retirees finish working and find the transition into retirement lonely, unfulfilling and unrewarding. Some even regret retirement. Living is always a challenge and our lives are constantly changing. We must ensure we are capable of remaining passionate about life and coping with the change life offers.

The feeling of isolation experienced by recent retirees leaving the workforce is not uncommon or hard to understand. One day you are fully employed with deadlines, meetings to attend and the next day you find yourself without this regimented routine. We spend our lives working towards the next promotion, and before long we are facing retirement without a clear understanding of what we are going to do with the next 20 years of our life.

Baby boomers have an opportunity to ensure they face retirement with a vision and purpose for what they wish to achieve in the second part of their lives. It is an opportunity to make a difference in the world. You must be the one who decides what you will do in retirement: if you don't, someone else will. Remember, you never get a second chance in life: this is it and this is as good as it gets.

Some people retire and find they have no interests. They may have worked their whole lives but they were never involved in any sports or other community activities and have gone through life without developing any leisure skills.

> *It was a high counsel that I once heard given to a young person — Always do what you are afraid to do.*
> – RALPH WALDO EMERSON (1803–82)

Momentarily consider your own life and think about the skills you have developed, or interests you have which are not related to your current employment. Do you spend your weekends cleaning the house, doing the garden, grocery shopping, watching TV, reading, being part of the cafe society or do you actively engage in leisure activities with other people?

Many of us have made our employment situation the main focus of our lives. Some of us may even spend weekends working on specific work-related projects. While there is nothing wrong with being a committed employee, it is important that you do not allow it to dominate your life.

Leisure is also an activity which needs to be practised. If you have spent your entire life on work-related activities, you will find the transition from work to retirement very isolating and difficult. It is also very important to interact with others of all age groups so you remain in touch with the younger generation and maintain social contact with your own peer group. Retirement planning is about creating a balance within your life. Remember the Money Karma Quadrant?

Start creating your retirement lifestyle while you are still working so that when you do finish working, you have many interests and you do not find retirement depressing and unrewarding. Don't limit yourself to what you already know. Expand your level of knowledge into new areas of interest and if you need some retraining, ensure you do it. Step out of your comfort zone and challenge yourself.

Start examining areas of your world you are passionate about. You need to ensure you remain an active member of society and you can only achieve this if you interact with others.

What is your area of expertise? Do you keep all of your information to yourself or do you assist the younger generation with some of your knowledge? Have you considered being an active member of a mentoring program?

Start writing down interests, causes, inventions or business ideas you could develop while you are still working and design a program so that you create your future now. You are capable of assisting in moulding a future that may benefit others. Some ideas include:

- Environmental care – forest regeneration/preservation, salinity, domestic water consumption and wastage
- Help a charity or a community service – Red Cross, Cancer Associations etc.
- Public Transport issues
- Develop a program to save and enhance the earth's decreasing resources for future generations
- Use your connections to develop programs that help the homeless, or help the younger generation into the workforce
- Start a business (but one that does not consume your retirement funds in start up capital)
- Help older generations with computer literacy
- Learn to play a sport, paint or play the piano

- Join a gym, go to a yoga class, or do other exercise
- Learn to fly a plane
- Take an art class
- Go to university – fulfil a lifelong dream
- Make a difference in someone's life with your assistance
- Lose weight
- Start a second career

The options available to you are limitless. Start doing something about your future life today. If you do, you will be able to make the transition from work to retirement without the added stress of completely losing your routine.

Age is something we cannot avoid and it is important we value each other's opinions, whether we're young or old. Life experience does not automatically come with age. Some of us may be turning 50 and have never travelled overseas, left our state, baked a cake, gone bush walking, driven a car, or done many other things. The younger generation may not have lived as long, but some have travelled extensively and developed an understanding of technology and how the world is evolving. Always ensure you listen to others, and just as you don't want to be judged on your age, ensure you don't do the same.

Challenge yourself by examining your current leisure activities. By this time next week will you have made an effort to research some areas of your life you would like to explore? If you spend your evenings watching hours of TV and hope for the best, you can visualise your retirement lifestyle – it will mean sitting where you are now.

How often do you go to social gatherings where you meet new people? Some people you find interesting and others you don't. Some will only be able to identify with issues that relate to their current employment. These gatherings are opportunities to

> *Don't part with your illusions. When they are gone, you may still exist, but you have ceased to live.*
>
> — MARK TWAIN
> (1835–1910)

> *Old age takes away from us what we have inherited and gives us what we have earned.*
>
> — GERALD BRENAN (1894–1987), THE BABY BOOMER'S BODY AND MIND

network with different people from different walks of life who you may find will be of value in years to come. An ability to interact with a wide network of individuals and relate to them on levels that are not limited to your area of expertise is invaluable. You never know when one of these contacts may assist you with retirement opportunities you may wish to pursue.

By developing alternative interests in your life besides your current employment, you are limiting the effects of unforeseen change within your life. If your spouse or partner leaves you, or if you lose your job, you will have other contacts and interests which may be able to assist you while you adjust to your new situation. You will find it easier to accept that life is always changing and nothing in life is constant.

You should now have a clearer understanding of how easy it is to neglect planning for your future retirement. Life is full of change, and retirement is a transition into a new chapter of your life. You don't want to live through a retirement filled with mundane activity. Once your life ceases to change and you no longer challenge your mind, you begin to lose zest for life.

Body

The changes experienced by baby boomers as they near retirement will not only include financial but also physical challenges. Your physical wellbeing needs to be a priority if you wish to enjoy a retirement lifestyle that is not limited by poor fitness. It is important that baby boomers challenge themselves daily by exercising and eating nutritionally balanced meals. It also means adopting a passionate attitude to life.

Everybody ages and retires at some time in their life. The difference between those who embrace life and those who don't is commitment and attitude. The only person who can ensure you have a fulfilling and rewarding life is yourself. With this in mind, it is time to understand the next chapter in your life is going to be entirely of your own making. If you are finding your life has no purpose or is becoming a mundane routine of experiences you find uninteresting, then change. Do something you wouldn't normally do. Being predictable is not a mandatory requirement for retirees.

Assess your current standard of fitness and overall wellbeing. Do you find you lack energy, and constantly feel you need sugar or caffeine hits to get yourself going again? If you are experiencing this lack of energy it may be time to become a little selfish, re-evaluating your diet and exercise regime. Your body may be lacking essential vitamins due to a diet polluted with excessive amounts of coffee, tea, chocolate and not enough natural vitamins and minerals derived from fresh produce and other foods. How many pieces of fresh fruit or vegetables do you eat a day? How much fat and alcohol are you consuming?

While many marketers promote the health benefits of certain alcoholic beverages they often fail to mention that alcohol obstructs the absorption of certain vitamins and minerals. When used in excess it can also lead to conditions such as liver cancer, cardiovascular disease and brain degeneration, and in some cases contributes to the effects of osteoporosis. Moderation is the key, and if you are finding you drink alcohol frequently no doubt you have noticed you feel a little dull the next day. You should ensure you have a few alcohol-free days every week as this will inevitably assist with your energy levels.

Preparing for your new lifestyle also means there are some physical obstacles which will affect relationships, including our financial ones. Men are often told that some time in their life they are going to experience a mid-life crisis. The symptoms may include a desire to colour their hair, get a body part pierced, buy a pair of jeans, buy a new sports car or other vehicle with excessive horsepower and speed. They embark on a quest to regain their 'youthful years' and some try to fight the reality that we all age by spending large sums of money.

It is different for women as they are constantly bombarded with messages that their mid-life crisis is due to an aging body which will require medical intervention to alleviate the symptoms – symptoms which may include hot flushes, weight gain, irritability and forgetfulness. While no one is refuting the effects menopause may have on some women, it does seem unfair that women are to expect physical and mental anguish while a male is only going to need to purchase a fast motor vehicle to satisfy his aging crisis. Unfortunately women only get a series of hormone replacement therapy pills and no excuse to spend vast sums of money on new feel-good purchases.

Researchers from around the world have documented that male menopause is a real condition. Like women, men need to understand that their bodies will experience a physical and mental change, which may affect their overall wellbeing and relationships. Men and women are going to experience financial and physical change possibly around the time they are planning to retire. Be aware of what to expect, and understand that it is a normal phase of life. Ensure you recognise and understand that your body continually changes and don't make any hasty financial decisions that you have not planned and budgeted for.

Mind

Retirement planning may be a confronting journey in our lives. We are presented with many issues, which at times may be overwhelming. It is essential you have some quiet time for yourself every day and this should include some form of mental relaxation, such as yoga or meditation. This quiet time allows you to feel inner peace, clearing your mind for the day ahead.

Adopting the Money Karma philosophy means you ensure you look after your finances, mind and body. These are the essential elements of life that enable you to function as a healthy human being. If you cease caring for yourself, you will have nothing left to offer others who share part of your life, including work colleagues, family members, friends, acquaintances and pets. The baby boomer generation is renowned for enthusiasm of spirit. Life is full of many experiences and you should never stop pushing the boundaries of enjoyment and learning. As we have said many times before, this is it, you don't get a second chance at life, so live it with passion and zest.

Summary

- Baby boomers need to make sacrifices in order to save the necessary income to fund their retirement.
- Some baby boomers will need to fund more than 30 years in retirement.
- Always save for a rainy day and don't live beyond your means.
- With an aging population governments will be unable to fund pensions into the future as they do today.
- Examine your current investment portfolio and ensure you have some investments which can be easily liquidated.
- Many baby boomers enjoy a high standard of living and many are not aware of the cost of their current lifestyle.
- Using the equity in your own home to buy dead assets (new TV or car), which do not generate any income, is unwise.
- As with any investment strategy it is important you understand the risks associated with your investment choice and the time frame for your investment as it is part of an overall plan to reach your retirement goals.
- The longer you procrastinate planning your retirement, the harder it will be to save.
- In the end it is your life and it is you who is going to live through the planning you put into your retirement.
- Set realistic goals and have achievable retirement goals to work towards.
- Unexpected external factors such as divorce, death or remarriage can impact on retirement goals.
- Your time to save for retirement is limited so it's essential you value every cent you earn and always live within a budget.
- Never make your employment situation the main focus of your life.
- Developing interests outside work will help you adjust better to retirement and to any other major changes in your life.
- It is important to take care of your body and mind to enjoy your retirement to the full.

Achieving Money Karma

There are two things to aim at in life: first, to get what you want; and after that, to enjoy it. Only the wisest of mankind achieve the second.

– Logan Pearsall Smith (1865–1946)

As this book draws to a conclusion you begin to understand your purpose of mind, spirit and soul, and the many pathways you can seek to fulfil your needs. It is now up to you to make the decision of actively changing your life for a new course which will create the experiences you wish to live through. Fewer than 10 per cent of people will make the necessary change within their lives to ensure they stop living a life filled with mundane activity and financial hardship. Money Karma enables us to remain focused to achieve our goals and not be sidetracked to pursue avenues that others have decided for us. When making life choices we must keep positive actions and outcomes clearly defined. Understanding that there is a consequence for every action and having purpose of mind helps us to remain focused. The Dalai Lama has said, 'A happy life is built on a foundation of a calm, stable state of mind.'

> *You must be the change you want to see in the world.*
> — GANDHI

Money Karma draws on the components of the quadrant of balance (page 18) – finance, family/personal, work and lifestyle – all of which are interconnected in your life. We use the same degree of energy, but it is our choices that decide whether the impact is negative or purposeful. Creating balance and happiness using Money Karma is about taking control and using money more efficiently, rather than allowing money to control our lives. Believe in yourself and your goals and do not be discouraged if you are not successful on your first attempt. Pick yourself up, dust yourself off (as the song goes) and start all over again.

Once you understand and adopt the concept of Money Karma you will no longer be burdened with unnecessary financial and emotional unhappiness. Your relationships with your friends and family will start to have more meaning but most of all you will not treat your money without respect. You will learn to value your time and appreciate the need to budget and plan for goals.

We hope you feel empowered by all that you have read about Money Karma. Appreciate that you hold all of the power for success. Self-discipline, consistency, persistence and honesty will lead you to your destiny.

As we seek our Money Karma pathway, continually sift the good advice from the bad. Spending less and saving more will ensure you achieve the happiness you deserve.

We wish our readers good fortune in creating positive Money Karma. May your new knowledge motivate you to do things well because of your human purpose of life and mind.

> *It is not the life you live but the courage you bring to it*
> — ANONYMOUS

Glossary

Asset Test A test that Centrelink apply to your financial circumstances to determine if you are eligible for government benefits.

Bad Debt Any debt acquired by purchasing a non-appreciating or non-income producing asset (for example, by purchasing consumer goods such as cars, boats, television sets etc. on credit).

Balloon Payment A large payment in a finance or lease agreement. Typically the balloon or residual is the last payment and is often 30–50 per cent of the purchase price (see **Residual**).

Cash card A card issued by your financial institution (such as your bank, credit union, building society etc.) that allows you to access your accounts electronically via an Automatic Teller Machine (ATM) or in-store through **EFTPOS**.

Cash Management Account An investment account offered by fund managers or investment banks typically offering at call returns above bank rates (often a minimum balance is required).

Charge Card A charge card is one that must be paid off in full at the end of every month. There is no limit on a charge card so you need to be very careful of how you use this card. The benefit of using a charge card is that you never have any credit card debt. It is also useful because you know that you cannot spend what you cannot afford to pay off. If you can't pay off the full amount you owe on your charge card you are in default. Access to the card is cancelled and the charge card company will take legal action to recover the outstanding amount. Charge cards are available from American Express and Diners, to name two.

Day Trading on the Stock Exchange The constant selling and buying of stocks on a daily basis with the goal of exploiting intra-day price movements for profit. This is generally regarded as a very high risk activity.

Debt Wisdom Debt wisdom means you are prepared for any unforeseen events in your life that may impact on your personal and financial well-being. It means you have a holistic approach to life, understanding the difference between good debt and bad debt and how easy it is to make the wrong financial decision. Debt wisdom serves the positive purpose of preventing us from reacting negatively to profound events in our life and the long-term consequences and implications – profound events such as the death of a partner, divorce, the birth of a child, getting married, moving house or making a poor investment decision. These events can impact upon our finances as we make drastic or poor decisions with our money to cope with these incidents.

Detoxify To cleanse our bodies of chemicals or substances that affect our health such as caffeine, alcohol, excessive sugar, fat, nicotine etc. (many people follow cleansing diets eating nothing other than fresh or uncooked foods or eliminating the above toxins from their diet).

Diversified Investments The concept of owning a range of assets across different investment markets to protect the investor from poor performance or investment failure in a single investment or asset class.

EFTPOS In-store electronic funds transfer system accessed through ATM cards.

Enlightenment An awakening of knowledge (the pathway to knowledge) and reality. Living with a sense of contentment, meaning, understanding and purpose. Finding 'the way'. You can never fully achieve enlightenment as life is a continual learning process.

Essence A unique element that makes something what it is. The core element of how something is formed. The embodiment of how something is constituted. A container for what is possible. An individual's essence is their personality, spirituality, humour and being. Your essence is what makes you who you are and what your dreams and desires are.

Fixed Interest Investments Investments in debentures or bonds, which typically provide steady investment returns. Fixed interest investments are medium to low risk investments.

Fixed Mortgage A mortgage interest rate set by your financial institution for a specified period. A specific interest rate for borrowed funds for a fixed term. You may not be able to make additional repayments.

Geared Investing The use of borrowed funds to buy investment assets that you would not otherwise have been able to afford (such as share portfolios and/or property investments).

Good Debt Any debt which is used to invest in income-producing or appreciating assets (such as shares, bonds and property).

Gross (Pre-Tax) Household Income The total income of a household before any taxes or expenses are taken out.

Growth Investments Investments that provide the investor with the opportunity for capital growth. Examples include Australian and international shares, and property.

Holistic Financial Planning The process of developing financial management and risk protection strategies that take into consideration all aspects of a person's life and goals, including lifestyle, health, family and finances.

Illiquidity The opposite of liquidity. Illiquidity in an investment means the investment cannot be sold quickly to convert it to cash. An example is real property.

Income Investments Investments such as debentures or bonds that primarily deliver income returns as opposed to capital growth.

Income Protection Insurance Insurance policies for individuals to protect their income in the event that they are unable to work because of injury or illness.

Index Weighting Indexes are used to convey to the public what is happening in various investment markets, for example the ASX 100.

Insurance Bonds A tax advantaged investment offered by insurance companies.

Interest Rate Yield Curve The interest rate yield curve describes the interest rates that are applicable over all periods to ten years (for example if you put on a graph the one, two three, etc. year interest rates, and then join the points, that is the curve).

Investment Yield The income return from an investment, usually expressed as a percentage.

Leasing (Hire Purchase) Leasing is a contractual agreement between a finance company and an individual or company, for the supply of equipment.

Liquidity The liquidity of an investment describes how quickly it can be converted to cash.

Listed Property Trust An investment that is divided into units or shares listed on the stock market, which allows small investors the opportunity to own a portion of properties such as Central Business District, commercial and industrial property.

Managed Funds An investment made up of a large number of individual investors' funds which are pooled and then invested into a range of different investment alternatives. Investors are allocated units in the fund and they can redeem their investment.

Money Depression The negative psychological effect of high levels of debt.

Money Juggler A person who pays one credit card off with another credit card while only paying off the minimum amount each month.

Money Karma Money Karma is the energy you draw from how you consciously manage your finances. It is an active energy that surrounds us all. You don't create Karma, it is there all the time, and it can be positive or negative, because there are positive and negative uses of money that either add to or detract from the quality of our lives. Money Karma involves the interrelationship between physical, spiritual and social elements and it requires us to balance many areas within our lives. Money Karma is a personal finance strategy analysing people's perception of happiness and what role they allow money to play in their lives.

Negative Gearing The investment strategy where the cost of funds exceed the investment income, reducing the individual's taxation liability. The strategy relies upon capital growth when the investment is eventually sold making up for the year-to-year losses.

Net Return The return from an investment after all taxes and expenses have been paid.

Phone Card An access card purchased from a newsagency or vending machine that has a monetary value that can be used in public phones.

Prepaid Phone Contracts Mobile phone contracts that have preloaded call values, so the purchaser does not receive a bill.

Property Syndicates Property syndicates are where a small group of investors pool funds in order to purchase commercial, industrial or retail properties. Typically the domain of experienced investors who can leave their investment in place for up to ten years.

Trusts Property trusts are similar to syndicates but the investment is unitised (that is, divided into shares) and these are often run as public offer unit trusts.

Residual Residual amounts often apply at the end of finance or lease contract and can be for 30–50 per cent of the original purchase price. (See Balloon Payment.)

Securitised When investments are securitised they are converted to property rights that can be bought and sold; for example mortgage monies.

Shares Publicly listed companies issue units (shares) in their business to investors at a price the stock market sets.

Sim Card A small chip that enables mobile phones to access a phone provider's network.

Socially Responsible Investing (SRI) The process of investing in a manner that takes into account the environmental, social, and corporate governance performance of a business.

Superannuation Superannuation is a retirement funding system designed so that people fund their own retirement income. Tax incentives are offered by government to encourage use of superannuation.

Time Horizon The process of matching the investment risk or maturity to the investor's goals.

Traded Endowment Policies Remanufactured whole of life policies that offer investors low volatility returns for a fixed period. Typically five or 10 years.

Wholesale Investment Options Fund managers offer lower cost investments if you are able to invest above a certain amount of money. These thresholds range from $100,000 to several million dollars.

Sources

Chapter 1
Zen Master Mazu in *Zen Essence, The Science of Freedom*, translated and edited by Thomas Cleary, 1989. Reprinted by arrangement with Shambhala Publications Inc., Boston, www.shambhala.com

Chapter 4
From Dennis L. Wilcox, Philip H. Ault and Warren K. Agee, *Public Relations Strategies & Tactics* (5th edn), Allyn and Bacon, Boston. Copyright © 1998 by Pearson Education. Reprinted by permission of the publisher.

Chapter 5
Gamblers Anonymous: www.gamblersanonymous.com

Chapter 6
Harding, A. & Percival, R. (1999), 'The Private Costs of Children in 1993-94' in *Family Matters*, No. 54 Spring/Summer.
Australian Nutritional Foundation – BMI chart reproduced with the permission of the Australian Nutrition Foundation Incorporated.
Financial Planning Association of Australia Limited – This material has been reproduced with the permission of the Financial Planning Association of Australia Limited. http://www.fpa.asn.au

Chapter 8
Suzuki, David: www.davidsuzuki.org
Greenpeace: http://www.greenpeace.org.au
UK Social Investment Forum – This material has been reproduced with the permission of the UK Social Investment Forum. http://www.uksif.org

Chapter 9
Australian Bureau of Statistics, 'Divorces, Australia Now: a Statistical Profile'. http://www.abs.gov.au/ausstats/ABS%40.nsf/94713ad445ff1425ca256820001
9af2/189dcccc4fe3b4deca2568a900154b0e. ABS data used with permission from the Australian Bureau of Statistics.

Acknowledgements

We gratefully acknowledge all of those wonderful clients who over many years have shared their personal experiences, which inspired us to write a financial planning book that examined physical, spiritual and social elements within our lives. Through their triumphs and failures we learned that successfully planning your financial future involves a holistic approach to how we live and achieve an overall sense of financial wellbeing. We thank them for sharing their stories so that others who read this book may now benefit from these life experiences.

We are both incredibly grateful to have such a knowledgeable literary agent, Lyn Tranter, for her belief in this project and professional advice. We would also like to thank Foong Ling Kong for her enthusiasm and the team at Hardie Grant for their effort, insight and guidance in making this book possible. To Jane Fitzpatrick, we would like to thank her for her time and effort spent editing this book. Our thanks also to Andrew Cunningham at Studio Pazzo for his design.

A special thank you to Heather Rickard for introducing us to the publishing industry and providing us with valuable support at the beginning of this project.

We would also like to thank those who inspired us and shared their information freely. These include David Suzuki, Gamblers Anonymous, the Australian Bureau of Statistics, Shambhala Publications, Pearson Education Inc., Helen Wildsmith from the UK Social Investment Forum, The Financial Planning Association, Professor Anne Harding and Richard Percival from NATSEM.

We would like to thank His Holiness the Dalai Lama for his spiritual wisdom and words, which shine throughout the world.

We would like to thank Katherine's mother Noelle for her tireless commitment and invaluable assistance throughout this book. Her encouragement, humour, support, and many hours of reading our manuscript made all the difference. Finally, thanks to our family, friends, and Kyton for their never-ending inspiration.

Index

A
accounting 50
allocated pension 184
annual fixed expenses 43
annuity 184
ASIA 107
assets 5, 10, 35, 60, 67, 94, 108, 109, 122, 124, 140, 145, 147, 159, 160, 162, 165, 169, 170–75, 193, 200

B
baby boomers 3, 144, 158, 161, 163–93
bad debt 49, 67, 68
balance 2–4, 10, 11, 13, 18–20, 40, 49, 50, 66, 86–90, 98, 100, 110, 117, 122, 128, 144, 155, 188, 196
beauty 46, 153,
beneficiary 122
Body Mass Index 99, 100
Buddhist 4
budgeting 6, 12, 37–53, 65, 72, 88, 91, 113, 150, 180, 211

C
capital gains tax 110
cars 5, 14, 15, 69, 80, 81, 130, 131, 159, 169, 172, 175, 183
cash card 63
cash flow system 38, 45, 48, 53
cash management account 73
CFP 75, 105, 107, 124, 183
charge card 49, 65
charity 42, 81, 96–7, 188
child support 42, 43, 94, 101, 151, 178
children 6, 14, 19, 26, 33, 59, 87, 89–95, 101, 119–22, 129, 136, 138, 140, 142, 145, 146, 147, 151, 152, 156, 161, 182
children's job list 93
Christmas 41, 42–3

comfort zone 12, 22, 36, 65, 73, 146, 188
conscious mind 20, 22, 23
couples 87–101
credit card 10, 13, 28, 48-50, 60, 72, 179
credit card debt 28, 29, 30, 39, 41, 42, 43, 57, 58, 62–6, 68, 75, 89, 90, 98, 109, 167, 169, 178–79, 181

D
daily expenses 46–52
daily fixed expenses 49
day trading 78, 82–3
de facto 135–37, 146, 149–50, 156
debt 5, 6, 10–11, 13–20, 35, 39, 41, 42, 44, 79, 83, 88–90, 98, 109–10, 123, 138, 143, 151, 156, 167, 168–73, 178–79, 181–82
debt reduction 25, 28–31, 49, 50
debt wisdom 55–76
destiny 3, 6, 17, 18, 20, 23, 25, 27, 33, 34, 36, 52, 57, 66, 68, 75, 81, 84, 109, 124, 196
detoxify 155, 200
Diploma of Financial Planning (DFP) 107
discretionary spending 52
diversification 5, 109, 114, 115, 117, 119, 120, 124
divorce 3, 42, 56, 95, 142, 145–47, 164, 165, 182, 193, 200

E
economic environments 34–6
education 18, 26, 42, 71, 72, 88, 89, 90, 94, 95, 120, 121, 122, 124, 136, 138, 141, 145, 151, 152
EFTPOS 63, 199
enlightenment 9–20
essence 22–3, 200
ethical investing 125–34

F

families 81, 83, 87–90, 90–101
financial adviser 62, 105, 173
financial destiny 3, 6, 17, 18, 20, 52, 66, 68, 75, 84
financial enlightenment 9–20
financial fingerprint 10
financial goals 3, 10, 12, 14, 150, 159, 179, 180
financial hardship 3, 6, 10, 20, 98, 136, 140, 143, 145, 149, 150, 196
financial wellbeing 6, 10, 11, 13, 56, 86, 98
fitness 3, 24, 164, 190, 191
fixed expenses 41, 43, 44, 49, 52
fixed interest investments 114, 185, 200
fixed mortgage 200

G

gambling 77–84
geared investing 67, 110, 200
goal setting 27, 28, 87, 88, 91, 101
goals 3, 4, 6, 10, 12, 14, 17, 20, 23, 24, 25, 27, 29, 30, 32, 36, 38, 49, 53, 57, 59, 60, 64, 67, 71, 75, 87, 88, 90, 91, 92, 101, 108
good debt 56, 67, 199
gross income 73
growth 68, 72, 86, 108, 111–24

H

happiness 2, 3, 7, 9–20
health 3, 4, 5, 11
holistic 56, 129, 149, 166
home loan 62, 73, 74, 171–73

I

illiquidity 201
income investments 108–24
income protection insurance 19, 74, 90, 111, 123–24
index weighting 128, 201
inner contentment 18, 20
inner conversation 32–3
inner empowerment 15
insurance bonds 117, 120, 201
interest rate yield curve 117, 201

investing 103–24
investment goals 118, 170
investment property 44, 110, 113
investment time horizon 118
investment yield 201

L

leasing 69, 70, 75, 201
liabilities 10, 35, 117, 143, 144, 149, 178, 181
life insurance 41, 42, 74, 111, 123, 124
liquidity 108, 111, 113
listed property trust 74, 111, 113, 114, 201
loss of income 35
lottery tickets 42, 80

M

managed fund 72, 74, 83, 115, 117, 119, 201
managing change 186–90
marriage 85–95
menopause 164
money depression 59–60
money graph 29
money juggler 60–1
Money Karma 1–3, 201
 Money Karma budget 3, 41–53
 Money Karma lifestyle planner 6
 Money Karma quadrant 5, 18
 negative Money Karma 2, 52
 No Fail Money Karma Budget 3, 41–53
 positive Money Karma 2, 20
money management 4, 5, 10, 13, 20
mortgage 3, 6, 10, 19, 26, 34, 41, 50, 59, 62, 70, 72-75, 81, 90, 109, 169–73

N

needs versus wants 52
negative financial energy 2
negative gearing 110, 201
negative Money Karma 2, 52
net return 110, 202
No Fail Money Karma Budget 3, 41–53

O
outward empowerment 15

P
phone card 71, 202
poker machines 80–1
portfolio 35, 42, 108–9
positive Money Karma 2, 20
poverty 136, 137, 158
prepaid phone contract 71, 202
property expenses 42, 43, 44

R
raffle tickets 81
real estate 35, 68, 106, 109–13
relationships 85–102
retirement 157–62

S
saving 3, 10, 15, 18, 42–9, 58–9, 71–3
scholarship funds 120
securitised 113
self-managed superannuation fund 185–86
self-discipline 2, 10, 11, 13–15, 20
shares 74, 108, 109, 111, 114–20
SIM card 71
single mothers 150–52
single women 152

slot machines 81
socially responsible investing 202
step-families 93–5
subconscious mind 21–36
success 2, 3, 6, 10–11, 15, 22, 25–32
superannuation 42, 137, 160–61, 168–69, 184

T
tax 15, 34, 38, 40, 51, 72, 73, 74, 75
tax effective investments 106
term deposits 117, 185
time horizon 118–19
traded endowment policies 120
trusts 94, 122, 202

U
unemployment 3, 35–6, 111, 144

W
wish list 16–17
women 89, 135–56

Y
youth debt 70–4

Z
zen 4

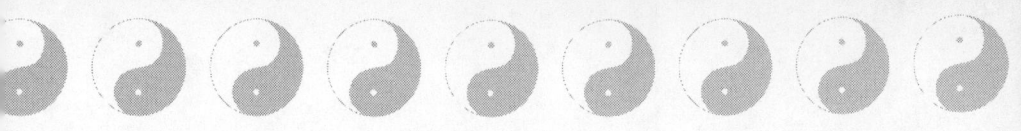

The Money Karma Lifestyle Planner on CD-Rom

Take control of your financial destiny with the Money Karma Lifestyle Planner, an interactive, easy-to-use software designed for you to create a budgeting system that will provide you with all the tools you need to organise your finances, including:

- the No-Fail Money Karma Budget Calculator
- Retirement Calculator
- Credit Card Debt Chart Calculators
- Child Budgeting Chart, including Education Funding Calculator
- Goal Setting Chart and Calendar
- Gambling Expenditure Chart and Calculator
- Investment Performance Calculator
- Baby Boomers' Lifestyle Budget
- Mortgage Calculator

For more information on how to order complete the following form.

Name	
Address	
Tel	
Email	

MAIL OR FAX TO:
**Jonathan Bonnett
Locked Bag 12
Southport 4215**

Tel: (07) 5591 0395   Fax: (07) 5538 5628
Email: moneykarma@moneykarma.com.au
Further information:
www.moneykarma.com.au

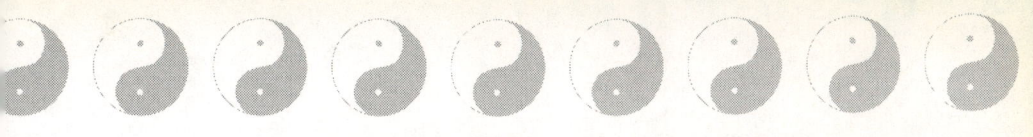

The Money Karma Lifestyle Planner on CD-Rom

Take control of your financial destiny with the Money Karma Lifestyle Planner, an interactive, easy-to-use software designed for you to create a budgeting system that will provide you with all the tools you need to organise your finances, including:

- the No-Fail Money Karma Budget Calculator
- Retirement Calculator
- Credit Card Debt Chart Calculators
- Child Budgeting Chart, including Education Funding Calculator
- Goal Setting Chart and Calendar
- Gambling Expenditure Chart and Calculator
- Investment Performance Calculator
- Baby Boomers' Lifestyle Budget
- Mortgage Calculator

For more information on how to order complete the following form.

Name	
Address	
Tel	
Email	

MAIL OR FAX TO:
Jonathan Bonnett
Locked Bag 12
Southport 4215

Tel: (07) 5591 0395   Fax: (07) 5538 5628
Email: moneykarma@moneykarma.com.au
Further information:
www.moneykarma.com.au